QUANTUM SPEAK
FOR PARENTS

GOLDYN DUFFY

Printed in the United States of America First Printing, 2020
ISBN 978-0-578-66148-3

www.goldynduffy.com

Acknowledgements

This book is a product of 27 years of working tirelessly to become the best mother I possibly could be. I could not have had the freedom and grace to live such an experience without my amazing husband, Michael Duffy. He has stopped at nothing to help us realize our dreams and to raise the ultimate family of unconditional love and joy. He accepted the burden long ago of being the sole breadwinner so that I could completely focus on being a wife and mother. He has taken on this role in such a way and become the big giant oak tree of support and strength through the lives of five women who have looked to him for his unshakeable faith and unconditional love throughout each one of our journeys.

To each one of our beautiful, strong, incredible daughters: our lives are what they are because of you all. We have grown and expanded along each one of you and because of that we are all stronger and more loving. I love each one of you with every fiber of my being and I have unwavering gratitude for your wisdom in my life. The things that I have learned being your mother and the wounds I have healed have helped me to become the strong, faithful, joy-filled woman that I am today.

To my grandbaby, Kinsley, for honoring me to be her Gigi. I am beyond blessed by this brilliant, beautiful being who has shown me more about unconditional love than I ever thought possible.

To BJ and Diane for being my unending support and creative team in making sure that my books reflect the creative juices that flow through me. Without the two of you I am not sure any of my words would have hit the world stage in such a fantastic and beautiful way. Thank you both for believing in me and the impact of the words that I write.

Contents

Quantum Speak for Parents

If you are a parent, odds are you have struggled at certain times of your parenting journey. Some of us struggle on a daily basis to feel that we are doing a good job and providing our children with enough love and attention to grow up and be good people. That's our intention. Right? I am sure you have had many days where you have questioned what you are doing and wondered why these little rascals can get you to lose your cool so often. I would often tell my husband that our kids could get the Dhali Lama to lose it. I had a strong belief when I was raising toddlers and teenagers (all of which were girls) that my life was a product of hormones and temper tantrums. I couldn't even imagine having a day when things were happy and joyful and I can honestly say wine o'clock was my favorite time.

Then one day, I went to a playgroup after a stressful morning of getting my teens to school and two toddlers to playgroup. I noticed that my girlfriend, who had a baby and toddler herself, was cool as a cucumber. I could just feel her energy. She was emanating peace and wait; was that joy?!! I was so intrigued that I begged her to tell me what she was doing. She shared with me that she started a meditation class that changed everything and I told her to "sign me up!"

Now you may have just glossed over the word meditation or had thoughts like, "oh I've tried that," or "really, that doesn't work for me." These were all things that I believed in the past and I think I overcame them out of sheer desperation. At that moment, I probably would have tried just about anything that even gave the slightest promise of parenting more effectively.

I realized at that point in my life that I did not like the energy in my home. There was a lot of bickering going on and even though my husband and I have always had a great relationship, I could often feel that we would try to top each other with how bad our day had been. I felt like I had to dump all of the girls crap on him in order to feel like

I wasn't alone and as an attempt to gain some sympathy from him. Meanwhile, he was out working super hard to support us, building a huge remodeling construction business that had tons of stress involved. We definitely weren't creating the most joyful existences.

I knew that I wanted things to change. I had a strong belief and could see that my energy was the strongest influence in our home. Now if you are a stay at home dad, I would say it's possible that you could have the strongest conduction of energy too. It's really the person who has the most influence for the most amount of time that creates the energy of the home. It's easy to blame our kids for their crappy energy or our spouse for the way they come home from work, but that kind of victim mentality needs to go by the wayside if you're going to take back your power and become the strongest force for good in your family life.

It is so easy as a parent to fall victim to our children's temper tantrums and challenges. We can allow these little beings, or big beings, to steal our joy and to create a life that feels less than joyful. It is up to us to understand that we are in charge of our energy, perceptions and attitudes and by taking on that new belief, we will have the most influence in changing all of our lives.

It is time for us to start showing our children that we will no longer allow feelings of guilt, shame or resentment to create in our families. The time has come for us to show our children that the better they feel and the kinder they are, the better their lives will also be.

I know it's not easy. Believe me, I've had years that felt like they would never end and like I was being tortured on a daily basis. I have found journals from when my girls were small, begging God to please help me be a better mother. I truly couldn't understand how these sweet little girls could make me crumble into a screaming, raging maniac that I didn't even recognize. I often couldn't believe the way I spoke to them or how angry I would feel towards them, and for silly things like sibling rivalry and messy rooms. Or how about when they don't listen? You can tell them to do something five times calmly, and then by the sixth or seventh time you feel like you have to yell in order to get anyone to hear you.

So, we may have been in the same boat at some point, until I jumped ship. That's right. At some point I decided that I would find a better way. I have done tons of research, seen therapists, cried, belly ached, complained, raged and discovered that everything that I was wanting to change had to come from within. I worked with energy healers and cleaned up my own stuff. I worked on my meditation practice and got to the bottom of my feelings that were contributing to the feelings of powerlessness. I discovered Universal Law and began working on my moment to moment energy exchange with my kids and I was absolutely astounded by my results.

I began to realize that my energy WAS the strongest force. I started to see how I felt about my children and myself was actually the biggest factor in what kind of energy was created in my home. I started to notice that as I found more peace and joy, that each one of my relationships with my girls improved along with my marriage. It still astounds me to this day. I often reflect back on that time period because it reminds me that I have control over how I conduct energy and that what I focus on expands.

1

UNIVERSAL ENERGY

We conduct energy based on our moods and our state of being. We can all feel the difference when we are light and joyful verses heavy and irritated. As we are conducting energy, people and circumstances around us correspond with that conduction of energy. You can think of it like a big radio station. Everything is happening around us based on the station we are tuned into. When we are tuned into frustration and aggravation, we will have less patience and find all sorts of things to make us feel even more short tempered. When we are tuned into appreciation, joy, and love, we will find we are tuned into laughter, fun, and silliness. Little things won't bother us as much and we will feel an ease and flow in our experience. We are tuned into a frequency that is lighter.

This is exactly why people who start the morning off on a negative note will encounter an entire day that feels bad. In order to get a hold of our state or be in charge of what station we are tuned into, we must be conscious and aware of our thoughts always, but especially **first thing in the day**. That is why becoming someone who is good at quieting the mind is of the utmost importance. Until you learn how to train your mind, you are subject to the 60,000 thoughts that you have had on a loop for years, possibly decades. When we allow our lives to be conducted from automatic behaviors and thoughts, we render ourselves powerless in a world that holds unlimited potential to become a deliberate creator.

Keep in mind, this is not an overnight, get calm, you'll never yell at your kids kinda book. This is a book that will give you the tools and resources to connect with your Higher Self so you can begin unraveling the journey of becoming the parent of your greatest potential.

It's not to say that you are not well on your way. The fact that you are interested in even reading about parenting says a lot about who you are and the potential you have to create a peace-filled, calm and loving home environment. The fact that you picked up this book means you have a strong desire to raise your family in a conscious way that allows for everyone to act upon their gifts and talents.

These methods are tried and true. I have used my own life experience to conduct experiments to see what works and what doesn't. I have struggled and researched and created a mess sometimes, of my own parenting journey, which I believe makes me a bit of an expert. I mean, I didn't quit. Even though there's been days where I wanted to and even considered running away, I would always find solutions to whatever I was facing in my parenting journey.

So knowing that there is this Universal Energy that is corresponding with the energy that you are putting out, can you see how you may be contributing to the temper tantrums and angst in your house?? If you could look at the energy that is flying around, what story would it tell you?? It's time to get real and to acknowledge that you have been just as much a part of the problem as you can be the activator of the solution.

2

LABELS AND JUDGMENTS

How do you really feel about your kids and what do you think and say about them? It's really easy to label our kids based on what we have witnessed about them. Our schools and doctors are extremely quick to diagnose our children with ailments that deem them less than or insist that they need to be on medication. There are so many kids out there that have lots of wonderful energy and they are told they are bad and have something wrong with them for it. I always find it very interesting that we expect little children with lots of joy and energy, to sit in a classroom and listen to someone talk for hours on end. How many of us adults could sit there and listen like we expect our kids to??

It's important to look at what you have been thinking and saying about your child because that is the station you are tuned into with them. If you have a child who you feel is difficult and you brace yourself when you have to deal with them, they will show you more reasons to feel that way. If you have a child who is easy and compliant, you will often feel calmer around them and less reactive. Now we could say it's because they are the way they are and that's why we treat them a certain way. This is true, sort of. In the world of deliberate creation, that kind of thinking will always take your power away. The bottom line is this child acts a certain way because you are tuned into that part of them. You are activating certain behaviors from them based on what you expect and how you are feeling inside. If you feel powerless and disrespected, then your child will treat you just that way. Now, you may be thinking, "Wait a minute, that means my kids are not responsible for his/her actions?!!" That's not it at all. If you are always making your kid wrong or pointing out what they keep doing wrong, I can imagine your relationship is not sunshine and rainbows. This is about you. This is about the frequency you are emanating and the way you are feeling that creates an effect in the energy of your family. Pay attention to the labels and judgments you hold about each person and then let's work on shifting those so you can tune yourself into a better station.

3

REMEMBER

I once had a dream when my third daughter was going through adolescence. In my dream she was three years old. I very vividly was able to see her in her innocence and silliness. I could see her sweet smile and hear her carefree laughter. I saw her in all of her brilliance and remembered the love I felt for her at that age. I woke up and felt better. I took out pictures of her when she was at this younger age and began connecting with her again on a different level. I wrote down lists of her positive aspects and looked for things that I loved about her. I took my attention away from her snarky, depressed attitude. We began communicating again and the energy between us felt lighter. She was still going through her roller coaster of adolescence, yes, but I didn't have to play a role that made it harder on her, or me. I decided that it was ok that she acted the way she was. I made peace with the fact that it was a phase and one I just needed to see her through. I reminded myself daily that it was all temporary and that I should never take the way she was acting personally.

Emma age 3. I often reflect on this picture to help me remember her sweetness and innocence.

If you are taking your kids moods and lack of joy personally, I would hope that this will shed a new light. I think it's really easy for us to get into the very bad habit of thinking our kid is doing things purposely to piss us off. The truth is they don't think about us as much as we would like to think they do. They really don't think about us much at all because they are incredibly self-involved. They do not have the capacity to ever put someone's needs before theirs and they definitely don't have the awareness yet to regard our feelings in any of the subjects that we think matter so much, like cleaning up after themselves or treating us kindly when they feel like crap. Remember, as children and especially as pre-teens or teens, their world totally revolves around them, and everything is extremely serious and possibly earth shattering. They haven't learned the art of allowing yet or believing that everything is always working out for them. They live in sort of an alarmist state, being super reactive and somewhat explosive depending on their hormones and brain development. You see, there are parts of their brains that are not fully developed that actually cause them to react instead of respond. Similar to a toddler whose frontal cortex is not fully developed to handle the vast amount of emotions that are coming forth, the teenager actually reverts back to that same temper tantrum display because they are not equipped to handle things differently. Also, they have not been taught that their emotions are healthy and can benefit them if they learn how to work with them. Heck, many of us are just beginning to understand the importance of our emotions. After you read this book you will have a much better idea of how to create space between your stimulus and response and I will give you some tips in working with your child on them as well.

This does not, in any way shape or form, mean that you should allow your child to have temper tantrum after temper tantrum and continue to disrupt the energy in the home in a powerful, negative way. This is about gaining your own awareness on your contribution and to infuse different energy when faced with a raging child, toddler, teen or anything in between.

4

MANAGING THE TANTRUMS

This is a simple guide to help you create the awareness you need to shift energy when you see it going awry. This is about you getting a hold of your own personal energy so that you do not contribute to the tantrum and make it worse.

Ok, so first you must know what you are dealing with. What is a temper tantrum anyway? Have you ever even considered this question? A temper tantrum is simply your child's response to stress and frustration. When they are super young, it's the only way they know how to express their feelings. When they become adolescents, they step back into a similar brain development growing period that they experienced as toddlers, so once again it is the only way they feel they can express their frustrations and feelings of powerlessness. The frontal lobe of their brain is not fully developed yet and is working hard to manage emotions that they are learning how to control.

As adolescents or teenagers, we see big people who should know better and can often mistake these taller, adult-like characters for adults and therefore expect way too much from them. We often expect our kids to act the way we would have and have the same feelings and judgments that we do because well, aren't we their role models?? The fact of the matter is, our kids are their own people and they have preferences and ways of thinking that are different from us. They may choose different paths and from our perspective, their judgment may be way off. But they must learn and be given enough freedom to make mistakes so they can figure out who they are and what they desire (more on this later).

In toddlers, these episodes take place more often when they are hungry and tired. Be sure to have a consistent schedule and for compassion's sake, please understand when your child needs sleep or food and meet their needs before it comes to this point. I think we all know what it's like to be *hangry* and we certainly know how awful we can act when we need sleep. So act accordingly and look at what may possibly have escalated their frustration so you can solve the problem quickly.

Please note, tantrums are not to be taken personally. Even in the adolescent years, your child is expressing emotions instead of letting them bottle up inside. When a teenager starts squashing their emotions, they may then start to look for other ways of unleashing their pent up emotions they feel they cannot share, like through drug use, cutting or other risky behaviors.

Some children can easily become overstimulated when their outside world is very busy or they have been in the presence of people. I would notice that my second daughter would often have meltdowns after parties or even after school. I believe certain kids have trouble navigating dealing with others and having to be on their best behavior for long periods of time. I find this is especially true for those sensitive ones who tend to run a little closer to their emotional fields. My daughter was hypersensitive to tags in clothes and even seams in socks were a nightmare. This caused us so much negative energy because I didn't understand and I wasn't aware enough to realize that she really felt these things more than others and I would take her battle to get dressed personally. Understand that if your child is on the sensitive side that you need to take more precautions and help them to navigate their emotions by giving quiet, alone time and compassion. It's important for them to know they are not getting in trouble and being sent to their room: they are being given an opportunity to recharge their batteries so they won't need to have a meltdown to do it.

5

POWER STRUGGLES

If you only learn one thing from this book, please let it be from this section. I set up lots of power struggles with my girls until I realized it was because of this deep down feeling I had that I was powerless. I realized that every time I would feel frustrated or upset with my girls, it was directly related to the powerlessness I felt about my own life. This is especially prevalent in the stay at home parent, who has put their dreams on hold to raise a family. It is easy to lose yourself in this role and feel like you have no purpose. Or maybe you are feeling powerless as the parent who is working a life sucking job just to put food on the table. Either way the feeling of powerlessness will really screw with your parenting game.

6

HEALING THE WOUNDS OF POWERLESSNESS

It's super important on this parenting journey to find ways to heal and become more in control of your emotional field. The best way I have found to do this is by quieting your mind. In Quantum Physics this is referred to as Zero State Awareness. It is in this state that you are given access to your old wounds and as you work within and heal them you are then given access to your power once again. The practice of quieting your mind is an integral part in becoming a happier, more effective and peaceful parent. Quieting your mind will help you to gain awareness around your triggers and the wounds that you most need to heal. It will help uncover many things that you have been frustrated about and help you to leave this cycle of frustration and create something much better. By creating space between your mind and your truest sense of self, you can start to uncover this amazing, limitless existence that helps you to step into your power and to parent from a place where you feel healed and whole and not fragmented and wounded.

7

PRACTICE

Quieting the mind is a practice that you will get better at over time. Find a quiet time and place in your day (you may need to create one by getting up earlier.) I promise it will be worth it and your day will run so much smoother! Sit up with your back supported by a pillow and be careful not to slouch or put your head back because you will fall asleep. Next, take a few deep breaths and begin focusing on your heart. Imagine there is a clear space that is allowing you to go deeper. As thoughts come up, practice breathing them out and coming back to your heart. I also like to imagine my mind is a blackboard that has been erased clean. I focus on the blankness of my mind and bringing myself to Zero State Awareness by allowing my mind to quiet. In the beginning, this may feel like you are taming a wild beast. The mind will give you many reasons to feel like you can't do this and it is in the overcoming of those thoughts that will eventually show the mind does not control you. Essentially you go behind the mind. You will experience moments, sometimes very brief, of complete stillness and bliss. As you continue to stay committed to your practice, these moments will get longer and stronger. Eventually you will see your practice bleed out into every area of your life. You will start to experience calmness and your mind being quiet throughout the day which will help you become present to life and joy.

8

DISCIPLINARIAN PARENTING IS OLD SCHOOL

If you take on the role of disciplinarian and corporal punisher, be prepared for a ride that will not only be bumpy but may lead to a crash and burn site. If your kids have no line of communication with you because you have set yourself on such a high pedestal from them, they may resort to risky behaviors. If they feel they can't trust you and that they will always get in trouble when they make bad decisions, you have severed the lines of communication that is necessary to be an effective parent.

You see, the old ways don't work anymore. Kids are no longer complying to what parents say because they have access to so much information. The corporal punishment days are over because kids are able to google laws and see how things are done differently in other families. We live in a faster paced world now than ever before, which means we must get smarter in order to heal our families and create a sense of peace and trust with one another.

9

KIDS ARE PEOPLE TOO

This is a really important thing to remember. Your kids are people too. They came to this journey with their own agendas, preferences, and guidance. They have feelings, and create beliefs dependent on what they have witnessed in the world. Since they formed their belief systems before the age of five, they may already have wounds that need healing and a skewed view of their world and who they are in that world. What they believe about themselves becomes evident as they move and respond to different things and show themselves evidence of what they have bought into.

10

THE SAME GOES FOR YOU

You also have belief systems that you have created before the age of five. The way in which you grew up and the beliefs you hold about yourself have very much created the life you live today. Is this hard to believe? You can't be a victim and know this. It's time to take back your power and start looking at these false beliefs you hold so you can stop the generational cycles that were put upon you. Do you often feel like you are acting like one of your parents?? Do you often hear your mother's voice when you are yelling at your kids? This is not about blaming your biological family, (although you may feel justified to) this is about waking up to the damaging, self-defeating, limiting beliefs that have brought you to this point in your life's journey.

We cannot acknowledge and recognize our own wounds if we live in a victim mentality. Your own journey has been a testament to many different unconscious people and the fears and low level beliefs they gave to you. Or maybe that's not you and you had a pretty perfect childhood and that makes you feel guilty. What I will say, is whatever your childhood was like will ultimately shape the person and parent you are today. It's your job now to go within and see what those feelings are and how to release the ones that are not serving you or your family.

If you have had a very challenging childhood with lots of abuse, you may want to examine this with the help of someone who can see you through the emotional healing process. I recommend someone who can help you release energy and come to Higher Perspectives. This will ensure that you won't get lost in the process or feel like you have no support. When you begin digging deep into wounds that have created a lot of triggers within you, it's important to know that you are not alone and to work with someone who will guide you to heal and find solutions.

11

MY CHILDHOOD STORY

I grew up in a pretty tough environment. I was the second child of three and my oldest brother was emotionally and physically abusive. He was like living with a big bully who despised me. I was the compliant one (until I became a teenager) who was always trying to please my parents. I got perfect grades, always cleaned the house, had to do various chores and did my best to behave. The problem was, I was constantly tortured by my brother, so I used to whine and complain a lot. I know I kinda sound like Cinderella here. Honestly, my parents paid me and there was always the feeling that I was the good child. I know that they loved me and did the best they could with what they knew. Unfortunately, their alcohol abuse and unconscious living did not serve me as a child or as a teenager. This definitely led me to lots of risky behavior and to a feeling that I could never go to them with anything. I so often felt powerless and it showed up big time when I became a mother. To the point where I would be an active member in the temper tantrum circus we all lived.

So I had to look at that shit. A lot. I had to dissect my own childhood and after a huge fight with my family that led us to an estrangement, I found myself in the therapist's office depressed and somewhat catatonic. I stayed this way for a few months before my husband offered me an alternative. He said, "either you snap out of this or I'm going to have to check out." Not meaning he would leave me, but emotionally he felt he couldn't keep trying to reach someone who was not there. Lucky for us both, that snapped me out of it. The type of talk therapy that I was doing brought up and had me revisit many awful things from my childhood. My therapists wanted to put me on medication and used the word "bi-polar." I decided that this type of therapy was not helpful. I found another therapist who had a different approach and helped me to start seeing the gifts I received from my experience and I started to feel better. Once I took my power back by deciding to work towards healing instead of talking about my past problems, I began to heal the brokenness I felt inside.

I think the bottom line is when you come from an abusive situation as a child, you set up belief systems that need to be released. You set yourself up with surviving mechanisms that can wreak havoc on relationships when you have no awareness around them. Awareness is the very first step in healing. Being aware of something doesn't actually change it, in fact, it can be darn right frustrating to be aware of something you feel powerless to change. This is why I will, ad nauseum, mention how important quieting your mind is to really create a significant change in allowing yourself to begin the healing journey that will profoundly impact yourself and your family. I would also suggest that if you find someone to work with, you make sure that after your sessions you are feeling cleansed and refreshed, not miserable and depressed.

12

VICTIMHOOD

Living in the past and regretting what your family life was growing up is victimhood. By blaming your mother, your father or your perverted uncle for things that took place in the past will only leave you with a feeling of powerlessness. By carrying around these resentments you will drag the past with you and continue to create that cycle in your life over and over again. So instead of having a brother who bullies you, you will find a spouse, a boss, a co-worker, or one of your children to commit the same acts that will prove to you how powerless you feel. Whatever you have not dealt with and allowed to heal within you will show up as cycles in your life and whatever generational bullshit you grew up with will continue in your family until you wake up and say, 'that's enough!"

I am living proof that you can heal from some crappy abuse. I have had phone cords wrapped around my neck and knives held to my throat, I have been scared for my life at times and I'm here to tell you that those wounds no longer affect me. My estrangement from my family is not something that happened because I am wounded. It was a decision I made after many dramatic events that I would no longer accept toxicity in my life. This decision is not for the weak and came with lots of grieving and heartache. I am in a place of deep forgiveness and a knowing that my path is not any less joyful than anyone else's. I love my family and I wish them the very best this life has to offer. I believe we are all better off on our separate paths and I have peace about that.

So let's take back our power, shall we? Let's make the decision today that the past is in the past and will no longer shadow our future. Let's seriously let that shit go. You deserve to live a life of joy and freedom. Untethering yourself from the years and years of stories you have believed and run over in your mind is one that will absolutely set you free. So what is it?? What memory shadows your life and creates in your day? If you don't know, I highly suggest getting curious. Sitting down, getting quiet and looking inside. If you are feeling angry, depressed, or frustrated, ask yourself what is at the foundation of those feelings and if you want to continue feeling that way. This is your journey and you get to decide how you will create. No one else has the power over you or the experience you are creating. So let's get clear, release some of those low level emotions and heavy energies and start creating from our whole, healed self.

Need help? I run a private facebook group with my amazing business partner, Jess Gumkowski, called the M21 Revolution. We guide people through the process of healing and mind training so that they can begin deliberately creating their lives. Go here to learn more https://www.facebook.com/groups/M21Revolution/

I also run a free group on facebook called The Real Onez with my soul sister Lisa Jones, where we teach deep spiritual and Universal Law practices in our everyday lives. Our website is www.therealonez. com and we offer lots of helpful tips and tools to support you on your journey to peace and love. Our show is also on YouTube. Please search Goldyn and Lisa The Real Onez and follow us!!

13

DISTRUST

When we were in the thick of it, raising our girls, there were many times we created from fear and distrust. I remember always thinking my older girls were lying to me and incessantly checking up on them. I would remember what I was doing at their age and assumed they were taking part in the same risky behaviors. I was terrified that they would make a mistake that could alter the course of their lives.

Brace yourself for this next story because it may activate a bunch of judgment within you, especially if: A. You have perfect children or B. Your children are still too small for you to relate.

When one of my daughters was 19 she was still living with us and I knew she was drinking a lot. She worked in a pizza restaurant/bar and I had an insatiable need to worry about her day and night. At the time

I had a policy that I would leave the light on in the kitchen and my older girls would turn it off when they got home. I have never waited up for them because I like to get to bed at a decent hour. She knew to come in and turn off the light and that way if I woke up in the middle of the night, I would know she made it home (seems kinda stupid now). Often times she would forget to turn off the light and I would wake up and worry and try calling her. Many times she was safe in bed and forgot to turn off the light. Waiting up for our kids to be home is an interesting concept, we deprive ourselves of sleep once again because of the belief that if we stay awake we will keep them safe?? I'm not sure but I never really bought into it and as a result my children have always returned safely. Recently one of my daughters had a problem in the middle of the night and we found out about it even though we were sleeping. Nowadays with cell phones it's even easier to know if they need us so staying up can be considered an old school practice.

This is the thing: I knew she was drinking and driving and it terrified me. We have had many family members create tragic results from drinking and driving and that always left me feeling so much concern for my daughter. In fact, my husband's cousin, (who was like a brother to us) died in a car crash in the middle of the night, so that haunted me. We got the call at 2 am, so whenever the phone rings in the middle of the night, we would always go back to that memory. This is how we create from past fears and experiences.

After a big snow storm one morning, my husband and I were cleaning off our cars and decided to clean hers off as well. We found a big bottle of vodka on the floor of her car. I remember yelling at her and telling her she was going to get arrested. She claimed it was her friends and she wasn't drinking. Ok, I wasn't born yesterday. So the fear continued.

After several months of not sleeping well and worrying about my daughter, an interesting thing happened. Now it's important to point out here that whatever we are focused upon, we will bring more of that into our experience. The reason for this is because of that big radio station we are tuned into. This is why it is so important to work through our fears and release them so we don't create from them. So one night at 2 am, I got a call. I ran to answer the phone, heart racing and so much fear running through my body. On the other end I could hear my daughter laughing and slurring her words. She had drunk butt dialed me!!! I was furious. I was so racked with anxiety and fear that I couldn't take it anymore. I was up for the rest of the night praying for a solution and feeling helpless and afraid.

The next morning I was totally exhausted and decided that I needed to make a change. I knew that talking to her wasn't working (tried that many times) and I also knew that if I shared all of my fears with her that I could possibly create negative scenarios in her mind, that would create in her life.

I know, I know, you may be thinking this chick is nuts and this book is not for me. This is some deep shit so I understand if you don't agree with it. The fact is, what I did worked for me. It freed me from massive anxiety and the worry and stress about my child. All of the worries we allow ourselves to feel for them, never amount to anything good. They never prevent anything from happening and contribute to the stress that takes us out of our joy. When we share our fears and the awful things that could possibly happen to them, we can introduce those things into their experience. Remember when I told her she was going to get arrested?

So that day I shifted into solution mode and the question that came to me was, "What if you just stopped thinking about it?" Huh? "What if you just let this whole thing go." What came to me was that there was nothing I could do about the situation physically so what if I just let it go emotionally. Stopped worrying. Stopped fretting. At first I didn't know if it was possible. And then after a few minutes of considering it, I felt a huge wave of relief rush over me. I could feel myself calming down and the anxiety subsiding. I knew that my daughter had her own journey and at this point I had done what I could to always keep her safe. I had prayed for her safety and that she would stop this risky behavior. I needed to trust the destiny of her life and to decide that I couldn't lock her up in order to ensure her safety. She knew what was right and wrong and would have to face the consequences of her decisions without my massive amount of anxiety creating in her life. I felt like a 1000 pound gorilla just climbed off my back.

A few weeks later she was arrested for drinking and driving. The crazy thing about it is, I was in California at the time and wasn't there to see her through her mistake. She had to learn it totally alone. I had energetically distanced myself so much from this problem that I didn't have to take part in it. So she dealt with it. She lost her license for six months and thankfully it was dropped from her record. She will never drink and drive again. Problem solved. Lesson learned.

I know this may seem like a crazy way to parent, but keep in mind she was older and at the point we were charging her rent for living in our home. She was acting like an adult in her everyday life and I knew that she knew what was right and what was wrong. One of the hardest things about being a parent is letting go and allowing your children to live their lives. Now if she was younger, I may have treated the issue differently because I was a different parent back then and was more of the disciplinarian who argued and punished. Having adult children living in your home is a different ball game, especially if they are paying rent (which they absolutely, 1000 percent should be), otherwise they may never be inspired to become independent and move out.

14

FAMILIES WHO HELP ONE ANOTHER

One of the biggest challenges I have found in parenting is getting our kids to do things. Right? LOL. Don't get me wrong, there are kids out there that are super compliant and want to help you always, but for the most part, especially as they get older, they don't normally really want to do anything chore related. Can we blame them? I mean, if we had a choice, would we do them? So the key here is to inspire them to want to help out or at least keep their room clean. Listen, I know it really bugs you. I know that it may drive you insane to allow your child to keep a messy room at all, especially if you're like me and you keep the entire rest of the house in good working order. So, how to motivate a child who doesn't care about a messy room or feel the need to ever clean it? Well, I have done a lot of ignoring of the messy rooms and when it really starts to bother me, I mention to said child that it would be so nice if their room was clean by say the weekend when they want to go out with their friends. That usually does the trick. Or if they ask me to bring them somewhere, I say I will drive you to the ends of the earth if that's what you want, *after* your room is clean. You have to be creative here and take the power struggle out of it. I no longer use a bunch of negative emotions and yelling to get my kids to do anything. I have found it's counter productive to create a power struggle over something that matters so little. I have had lots of talks with my girls about how much better their lives will run when their rooms are organized and that works, sometimes. Because I don't have boys, I'm not sure if that kind of talk will work but I do know insisting that they clean their room before you drive them anywhere is very workable. The important thing is how you approach this and how you feel. If you feel powerless and frustrated with this messy room you will only create a power struggle and invite in a bunch of resistance. By relaxing and being more casual about it, very matter of fact, you will see results faster.

If your kids are small, sometimes a super messy room is overwhelming to them. I would either help them do it or ask them to clean a corner at a time. If they have too much stuff, then I would highly suggest getting rid of some stuff to help them manage things easier. The way to do this is to share that no more toys will be bought until some that aren't being played with are given away. This way, you keep them accountable to releasing things they are no longer playing with and give them to kids who will love them again. Remember Toy Story? If not, I highly recommend you watch it with your child and explain how toys deserve to be loved and if they're not, it's time to let them go where they will be appreciated. I also used to suggest that they tidy their rooms before going to sleep at night sharing that it will help them sleep better and wake up in a better mood because things will be organized. This was a great way to help them maintain their room so it wasn't such a big job.

The most important thing when it comes to chores is to realize that they do not make or break your child. You are not setting them up for a life of laziness or messiness. Chores are a way for them to manage something that at times in their life feels very unmanageable and super unimportant.

When my older girls were small, I was crazy about the house being clean. I would have huge temper tantrums over messy rooms and chores not being completed. I can see how that was not only a waste of energy but many times ruined the energy in our home. Especially before a party or a holiday, I had unrealistic expectations around needing to look perfect to my relatives which created lots of stress for no reason.

Don't get me wrong, my house is super organized because that is the way I feel my very best. If the kids leave stuff all over, I will always ask them to clean it up (without the demanding, harsh energy attached to it). I simply say, "Please clean up after yourself" and this usually works. If it doesn't and they forgot, I may mention it again and if it's still not done (which doesn't usually happen) I may just take care of it. The secret here is all about the energy and what you are conducting when asking. If you have a strong belief that your child never listens to you and an underlying feeling of powerlessness, you will definitely have trouble making this ease and flow way of family life work for you. It's time to get to the bottom of those feelings and beliefs and make a decision that you will move away from the thoughts that keep this situation creating in your life experience.

I highly recommend starting these healthy practices when they are small and remember your kids will follow your lead in some ways. If they see that you are always leaving your dirty clothes on the bathroom floor and your room is a disaster, it will make no sense to their logical mind why they should have to behave differently. If you have decided that this is just the way you are in life, then you probably should accept that they may take on these habits as well. I understand that some people may feel this is a perfectly fine way to live but I would also challenge that belief system by saying if you live like this, try it a different way just for a week or two. A well organized home has better energy flowing through it and will help you to not feel so overwhelmed when life is giving you lots of reasons to feel that way. When you are doing a few minutes of tidying up throughout the day, you will be able to find things more easily and you will create an overall feeling of calm in your household. If messes do not bother you in the least, then I guess you probably, or at least hopefully, don't have issues with your child being messy because they may follow your lead.

15

CHORES

When my older girls were younger, I kept a very detailed chore sheet and used it to modify their behavior. I believed that using a chore chart was a great way to keep our house running smoothly. My belief has always been that we all reap the benefits from a well run household. At the time I was seeing a Psychologist by the name of Thomas Houle. He had worked with troubled boys and had a fantastic system for helping children to behave. The key to his chore system was listing different jobs and behaviors and giving each chore a number. If they didn't do it you would simply circle the number and dock it off of their weekly total. The secret to the success of this chore chart was simple: you couldn't say anything. The reason for this is because if you engage with them, you invite in a power struggle. At the end of the week you tallied up their numbers and a certain number enabled them privileges. Like play dates or ice cream dates. This was the best chore system I have ever used and it worked as well as I was at working it. The problem I see with chore charts is consistency. If you aren't consistent with it, and don't put in the work it requires, your whole system will fail. So I did this for a while and it really worked. Then I stopped ... and it didn't. With my next two children, I decided to forego the chore charts and use conversation and reason. This works really well with certain children. I would express what my needs were and then discuss why it was important to me. When they were younger than adolescence this worked well because they were still in the phase of pleasing me and they didn't enjoy it when I got mad at them and then at myself. As they get older this doesn't always work. Once again I found myself in a position of allowing them to keep a messy room and their own piled up dirty laundry. The interesting thing about this is, my younger one, who has a super busy schedule, will just randomly clean her room because she likes it clean and my third daughter always keeps her room clean because she likes it that way. I didn't have to fight for this and it has made our house run a lot smoother. I think because I haven't made it a power struggle they have come to their own understanding that they are happier when their rooms are organized.

There is nothing wrong with wanting to teach your kids responsibilities and also having some help around the house, especially if you work outside the home and can't possibly get everything done by yourself. I like conversations that communicate teamwork and provide your children with the knowledge of what you face on a daily basis. Let them know how stressed you feel when things get out of control at home and share that you are out there working hard for them. Help them to understand that you know doing chores sucks and you aren't a fan either. If there is a chore they really despise doing then maybe trade it for something else. Or teach them the art of mastering something they don't like by changing the way they think about it. We can do this for ourselves too. Like for instance, let's say you HATE cleaning out the dishwasher, what can you do to make this chore less disliked by you? Can you turn on some good music? Can you do it as a family (one person, does silverware, another does plates, and another does glasses?) Any chore can be made less painful by the way we are thinking about it. You can actually love washing dishes if you become totally present and realize that doing the dishes actually forces you to slow down and breathe. Feeling the warm water on your skin, removing all the food, rinsing the dishes that lovingly held the food you all ate can be an expansive experience into more joy, if you will allow it to be that. You can teach these practices to your kids too, as long as they are open to listening. I even like the idea of brainstorming with them to see how you all could look at chores differently. Like while you are cleaning the litter box can you think about how happy your cats are everytime they have a clean box to go in?? Or every time you walk the dog and have to pick up their poop, can you look around at the beauty of the sky or focus on the relief your dog feels that it is outside and relieving itself? I know I may be crossing over a line here into Pollyanna land that you are rolling your eyes at, but seriously what do you have to lose in looking at life's monotony with a fresh new perspective?

An important piece to note here is to compliment and notice when your children do pitch in and help with the housework. If your tendency is to complain about the job they did or tell them how to do it better, they may not be excited to do it again. When we notice and thank them, it helps them to see that the chore that they think is pointless, actually makes a difference that is noticed and gets them some positive attention.

16

TUNING YOURSELF INTO JOY EVEN WHEN THE JOB SUCKS

The winter before we moved to California, we experienced a ton of snowfall in Connecticut. Because our driveway was short with no place to plow the snow at the end of it, we would always have to shovel it. This was about a two hour process (sometimes all day if we got a huge storm), and it was always something I totally dreaded. I like to refer to it as nails in the coffin of living there. You see when you are very unhappy about your life circumstances, you are creating a lot of desires that can help you activate the solution. If you are miserable, you are living in the lack of what you want and will most likely stay there until it gets so bad you can't take it anymore or until you can shift yourself into a place of not feeling so stuck. So I made a decision. I decided that I had been living in the lack for too many years and I needed to shift my thinking if I was ever going to create the epic adventure of moving to California.

I decided that I would embrace shovelling. I put on some great music and I danced all over that snow until it was gone. I couldn't believe how fast the job went and this is the most fascinating part of this whole thing: I wasn't sore from shovelling. Normally my back would hurt for the rest of the day, and the next day, I would be super sore. I figured out that by being in a high vibrational state and feeling good while I was doing it, I escaped all of the physical detraments that I would normally experience when I was creating misery while doing it. Your mind will activate your field and how you are feeling. Your thoughts, your mood, and your attitude decide what you will experience next. This is the thing about Universal Law, it responds to how you are feeling. If you are feeling happy, appreciative and light, it will respond by giving you more reasons to feel that way. You will be less likely to catch colds and experience other things that are annoying. Often times things may happen and you may wonder why you attracted such things and maybe even try to blame yourself, feeling confused why something happened. The Law of Attraction is not what comes to you but more about how you respond. Your response is what you are actually vibrationally aligned with.

17

REACTION VS RESPONSE

One day I was driving in NY and I was feeling so good. I was doing business in town and life felt light and joyful. I came to a four-way stop and apparently went before someone who felt they should have been able to go first. This man started yelling at me and flipping me off and I thought, well why the heck did that happen? My next thought was only to throw him a kiss, like genuinely because I felt like he could use some more love. The Law of Attraction is not necessarily what happens to you but more about how you respond. If you are very reactive and fly off the handle at little things like crazy people, well that just means you weren't in as good a place deep down as you thought you were. Your reactions will always tell you where you are conducting energy from. They will always tell you how you are truly feeling inside.

So if you are super reactive to your kids, it's ok. This is just a symptom of the momentum you have been allowing. Once you know this information you can start to take hold of your life and put an end to creating by default. You can take control back over your mind and your life. You can start deciding how you want to create and then your world will start to take on a whole new energy.

Understand that you have had a boatload of momentum going in a certain direction with your family. You have had things set up for awhile so it may take some time and some space to begin to shift the energy field. If you have always been a yeller, well congratulations on reading this and looking for the solution. Honestly, yelling does the exact opposite of what you are trying to accomplish. I know in the moment it feels necessary and well, down right good to allow your frustrations out and let this heavy energy out of your body. I also know that you may not feel you have any choice about it. The truth is, we absolutely always have a choice and just because you have chosen to be the screamer parent only means that you may have an even stronger desire than most to figure out another way. I was definitely a screamer when my older girls were younger. Not like a public screamer but when we are at home and no one could hear, I would unleash all the frustrations and powerlessness I felt on a daily basis. I would allow messy rooms and children who wouldn't listen to drive me to the point of crazy town, where I would see no way back except to lose it. I would feel absolutely awful after, the feelings of shame and guilt just further drove my feelings of powerlessness. When I was acting as this unconscious parent, I could never see my kids point of view or explain to them why clean rooms and listening were so important to me. I'm sure they felt confused and even though I thought it would create some sort of action in them, it was nothing that was long lasting or created any kind of peace in our home.

It wasn't until after I started my commitment to quieting my mind that I stopped this insanity. I started to wake up as a parent and to see how my yelling was only further solidifying the behaviors based on the fact that I was so focused on noticing what wasn't working that I created way more of it. It finally clicked to me what all those parenting books were talking about when they said, "Ignore the bad behavior." Whenever I would read that I would think, "yeah right, you don't live here, that's impossible." And because of that belief, it would be years before I would realize and come to the knowledge that "what you focus on expands." By always focusing on what your children are doing wrong or not doing what you want them to do, you will activate more of that in your experience. The reason for this is because of the energetic output you are conducting when you think certain ways and feel so fed up with your children's behavior. You are literally tuning yourself into the station of non-compliance. The reason for this is because statements you have made or thought like, "No one ever listens to me," and "I can't take this anymore." Remember the old Calgon commercials? We have literally been programmed as parents to need something to take us away. If you have had moments or even an underlying feeling like you can't stand things anymore, you are creating an energy in the Universe that will give you more reasons to call on Calgon throughout time spent with your family.

18

LAZY PARENTING

Ok, so if you're quick to be offended, you may want to check yourself before you read this part. I see a lot of lazy parenting out there and parents who are so overwhelmed with surviving that many of our kids are not getting their emotional needs met. If you never talk to your kids, take any interest in them or engage in conversations, you will put yourself and your family in a losing position. When kids are little they need structure. They need to know where the boundaries are and they need to learn that they will not get their way when they are exhibiting negative emotions. If you do give into them when they are creating negatively, you will teach them that this is how life works and that is a terrible disservice. My advice here is to NEVER give in when they are having a fit. If they are begging you and carrying on and you already said no, they must exhibit better behavior before you allow them to do whatever it is that they wanted to do. Do your best to not say no to everything and really consider what they are asking before you answer. I always say, "let me think about it" so I can decide from a conscious place and not just spout out "no" because that can be an automatic response. Once you say no, it's not a great idea to change your mind because that teaches your child that they can beg incessantly or pitch a fit and then you will change your mind. I am pretty firm once I say no and that is why I really think about it before I say it.

When it comes to your younger children, the way I see **lazy parenting** is when you yell at them for having negative emotions or you give into them so they don't freak out. Now, I know temper tantrums are a bitch. They happen at the most inconvenient times and seem to shred our nerves like no other thing on the planet. This is why meditating and being super conscious and aware is so important. The cleaner you can keep your energy and the higher you can maintain your high vibe no matter what is happening around you, the less these temper tantrums will rule your household. If you are having temper tantrums alongside your child, just know you are human. Learning to manage the vast amount of emotions we have in the face of adversity is seriously expanding and big growth stuff. When you realize deeply that you are a serious role model for your child you will have the desire to work on your stuff so you do not pass it on generationally. This is why I recommend a quieting your mind practice. Just 15 minutes per day can make a huge difference in the management of your emotions. This practice also will help you to create more awareness and begin the process of healing from the traumas of your past. You will uncover so much about yourself and when you can really dig down and see where your emotions/feelings and beliefs come from, you begin the process of deliberate creating.

Now you may believe that you can't do it. Your mind is too busy. I hear it all the time. This is a belief that will kill your practice. Yes, that's right I said practice. You have to practice to get good at it. Your mind is like an untamed wild beast and when you first try to tame it, it will get stronger and scarier until you stand up strong and decide that you will no longer be a victim to your mind. Once you do this, you will start to have breaks of thought, which you may not be totally aware of, that you will receive great benefit from. Soon, maybe after seven days of this wild animal mind taming, you will find yourself in moments of nothingness. This is what I like to refer to as pure bliss. Quantum Physics refers to this as Zero State Awareness. It is in this place where all creation begins. Meaning we have the most power in this state because we clean our slates and allow that wild animal, the mind, to lay down and be quiet. Once our minds are quiet we begin to create a relationship with our innermost selves. That deep place within that allows us to uncover our power and our truth. I know this may be a weird concept if you have never lived a second without your mind telling you who you are, but I promise once you stick with the practice, you will gain a lot of clarity about your relationship with yourself. Some refer to this as your soul, your inner being, your spirit. I like to think of it as the stream of energy of All That I am, which is connected to the stream of energy of All That Is. Without getting too technical, you may think of that as God. The only reason I don't use that terminology is because I like to steer away from anything you grew up with that may cause you to think a certain way about this Stream of Energy. My goal here is to assist you in seeing that you are not separate or disconnected from this Stream of Energy but in fact an expression of All That Is. Regardless of what you believe and how my terminology may make you feel, I ask that you stay open and anything that doesn't feel right to you, you can leave as not for you.

This field of energy is here for you and will be at your assistance anytime you call upon it. Whether you call on God, the Angels, Universe, Source or whichever way you like to think of it, we can call It in whenever we feel we need the extra help or protection for our children. I love living with this philosophy because it allows me to be free from worry and invites me to trust in my own well being and the well being of my children. I also like to use it to help me find things that are lost, or to help me find parking spaces. In the field of Quantum Physics, this is about wave conduction and allowing your wave of intention and belief to conduct in the physical.

19

THE SCIENCE

Whoa, you may have thought I slipped off my rocker here for a second. I like to explain the Science of Creation to help you further make sense of your life and the energy that you are emanating. So you have a *thought*, that is backed up by a *feeling* which is created by a *belief*. This three fold system creates a wave of energy that goes out into the Universe and **if it is strong enough, meaning you have dialed into the frequency of it by thinking about it and feeling for the energy of it, you emit a frequency that is then broken down into particles and becomes matter.** Once this happens, these waves of energy then begin to take on physical characteristics that you will then start to see evidence of. Ever think of someone and then you bump into them or they call you? That's the energy of what I am explaining. Some like to refer to this as the Law of Attraction. I like to think of it as the Law of Correspondence. What you are sending out you will get back. So what does that have to do with raising a peace-filled family? Everything.

Your children will respond to you based on the frequency that you are emitting. If you are emitting stress and frustration, they will give you more reasons to feel that way. Ever bark commands at them and down right treat them with disrespect? Guess what's coming back to you? Yup, a boatload of disrespect. I remember when my kids would do things like spill something on the carpet and I would scream at them and then my friend would spill something on the carpet and I would be like, "That's ok, accidents happen." Huh? Here are my children that I brought into the world, who I love more than anything and I am treating them like they are absolute dirt. Why is that? I had to get curious before I found the answer.

After much study and reflection, this is what I found. There is this thing called momentum. When you have had a lot of momentum in a certain direction, it is super easy to lose your cool and yell at your kids. When they have done things to trigger certain feelings in you over and over again, it is super easy to be reactive. How do you stop momentum? Well this is where our good old friend mind training comes into play. The more time you can spend quieting your mind and interrupting thoughts about how awful your kids are and how bat shit crazy they make you, the more control you will have over things. After awhile you will find yourself more at choice and you will be able to respond to your kids spills and antics just like you do your best gal or guy pals. I'm not saying your kids need to become your best friends or anything but I will say when you get cards from them that say you are, it certainly does feel super amazing.

So the secret to halting momentum from shitty reactions and feelings about your kids is all about awareness first. Awareness will not necessarily change your response but it's the beginning phase in gaining control over your energy conduction and creation. Once you are aware then you can begin to interrupt or choose how you want to feel and how you will respond versus react. If I find myself in a harsh reaction to my kids (no one is perfect all the time and hormones happen) I find no problem in apologizing to them and explaining what brought me to the brink of joining the temper tantrum circus. Then I will go within, look at what the foundations of my feelings are and why I feel so reactive to this particular incident. Does it make me feel powerless? Do I need to be in a power struggle over this? And how helpful is this battle I have set up with said child? How do I want to feel? It is asking these questions that really helps halt the negative momentous feelings in their tracks. Once I have enough awareness to formulate this question, I know I am three feet from the gold of solution energy.

20

OUR BELIEFS MANIFEST

We create our own reality and what we decide about our children does manifest. My youngest was a thumbsucker. She carried around this little bunny blanket called Boppy. From the time she was a few months old, this little bunny went with her everywhere. Boppy had been torn to shreds and sewn back together many times. He had also been left in parking lots and found more times than I can count. We always found Boppy and her thumb provided much needed self soothing that was helpful for being the last of four girls. Many people told me their stories about why I shouldn't let her do that. They said thumb sucking was germy and she would have buck teeth as a result. People around me would tell me I should put nasty tasting stuff on her thumb and pull it out of her mouth whenever I caught her doing it. If your child is under the age of 5-6 and needs a sucking device, whether it be the thumb or the pacifier, I hope that you would allow them the simple pleasure of self-soothing. Your child has their own guidance and yes, despite what your mother-in-law/friends/relatives like to believe about them sucking their thumb into their late teenage years and ruining their teeth, it simply doesn't have to be true. I refused to buy into any of that. I trusted my baby girl to use her own guidance and lo and behold, she stopped when she was ready. I didn't set it up to be a problem, so it never was. Her teeth grew in perfectly straight and she gave up thumb sucking all on her own around (I think it was) the age of six. It was so not a big deal that I don't even remember. I just remember her feeling like she didn't want to do a baby thing anymore and it falling away naturally. I do find Boppy in her bed occasionally even though she's 15, but I actually love that and I never find her sucking her thumb anymore.

My sister was a thumb sucker and my parents had a very different approach. They shamed her for it and put stinky things on her nail. They told her it was for babies and it would ruin her teeth. Don't you know she had a really hard time giving it up. In fact, I remember when she was ten years old, sleeping with a sock on her hand so she wouldn't accidentally put it in her mouth when she was sleeping. She also ended up with braces and all sorts of other dental devices to straighten out the teeth her thumb sucking ruined. What we focus on becomes, people, in real, true form.

21

ENERGETIC FOCUS

When one of my daughters was in her late teens, she had a boyfriend
that we severely disapproved of. I swear everything that came out
of his mouth- I wanted to stick my foot in it. He was negative and
someone I completely distrusted. As much as I tried, because I am a
firm believer in supporting our children's decisions, I could not make
myself like him. This went on for a few weeks and since it was the
beginning of my journey of studying Universal Law, I decided to try
a little experiment. I never spoke of my disdain to my daughter and I
invited him over for dinner and did the best I could to tolerate him. I
spent no time worrying that she would end up with him and I actually
decided that he would go away because I wanted him to. One night,
while we were at a concert with our family, he had borrowed her car
and got into an accident with it. His response was to yell at her and
tell her it was her fault, even though she wasn't there. See, I told you

he was a jerk. She immediately decided she was too good for him and dumped him that night. My experiment worked and helped build my confidence in my power to create.

So our kids will do things that we don't care for and they may even date people we can't stand. The bottom line is energetic alignment and focus upon what we want is way stronger when we don't create a lot of resistance around it. If we had set up a power struggle with her, she may have stayed with him for longer just to prove her point. She's always been our super strong willed child so parenting her has taught us a lot about letting go and allowing her to follow her own guidance. Whenever we would create a power struggle with her, we would all end up losing. Losing communication with her, forcing her into risky behavior, and creating an energy that was a battlefield.

22

STRONG WILLED CHILDREN

So you have been granted a strong willed one, huh? Congratulations.
They will teach you more about letting go than any other children you
will have. They will help you heal every wound and trigger faster than
any other trauma you have experienced. They will bring you to your
knees on many occasions and absolutely make you think you are losing
your ever loving mind. So why am I congratulating you? Because
if you have a strong willed child it means you are a freaking warrior.
That's right. It means you have the capacity within you to rise up
against the belly of the beast. If you didn't have what it takes, they
would never have chosen you to raise them. You would not have been
entrusted with such a powerful strong little being if you didn't have
the strength and resolve to rise up and meet that power with the most
powerful force on the planet: unconditional love.

Your strong willed child is not here to break you. They didn't come here to make your life miserable or to put you in the crazy house. They are here to teach you, to help you wake up in the most powerful way possible. These exquisite beings need a whole different approach when parenting and luckily we usually only get one in the bunch. If you have more than one then I would say your strength is even more extraordinary. Luckily, I had one and she has turned into the most amazing adult and mother. And for karma's sake, she may have a strong-willed one on her hands as well. Not to say that I wish any type of negativity on her life, because I know she has the strength and the ability to handle whatever my sweet grandbaby decides to awaken within her.

Strong-willed children need choices. They need to be empowered on a moment to moment basis and if you set them up in a power struggle you will most likely lose, every freaking time. When it comes to eating, sleeping, and doing school work, you need to find what works best for them. Forcing and yeling at them will only create more stress and less production. They need firm boundaries but also need to feel that they have some say over their lives. Communication is key with these types of people and letting them know that you understand their inner will and you respect that they have their own guidance. It is very important that you ask them how they feel about things and empower them to make good choices by presenting them with choices and that you are not constantly telling them no. Because they will relentlessly beg until you are so worn down you will eventually cry for mercy. So take time before you answer them, make sure no has to be a no, and make sure you offer choices to help them feel like they have some say over their lives.

Communication is truly key here and asking them how they feel. I know, old school philosophies do not agree with this at all. The notion that we are giving our kids too much power and entitling them is bullshit. If we treat them with respect and help them to tap into their own guidance, then how in the world can they feel like the world owes them anything?? I have heard people say we are talking to our kids too much and asking their opinions devalues our position as parents and to this I would also say, that's crap. I have seen it with my own kids, when I open the floodgates of communication, we always win. We create pathways to solutions and everyone feels heard and respected. I know from experience that working as a disciplinarian with a strong-willed child will have the cops at your house more than once. Believe me and let me save you from that type of drama. It's not worth it and it does not work. Unless you are trying to drive a wedge between you and your child. Which I'm guessing is not the case, since you are reading this book.

Strong-willed children do much better with consistency and structure. They need to be in bed by certain times but not necessarily asleep if they are not tired. If they can't wake up the next day, then the lights need to go out sooner. Certain things can be helpful like having them listen to guided meditations or soft soothing music. These types of kids have trouble quieting their minds so something soothing like a nice hot bath or reading a book could help them fall asleep faster. I'm also a big fan of sleepytime tea or using Lavender oil to help relax them. I know it's easy to become frustrated with these little night owls as you may feel you can't actually relax until they are sleeping, but please know that they are not staying awake to drive you crazy. Could you imagine if someone yelled at you every time you had a hard time falling asleep? Yikes! That certainly wouldn't help you fall asleep any faster, in fact it would most likely create an anxiety that would make it even harder.

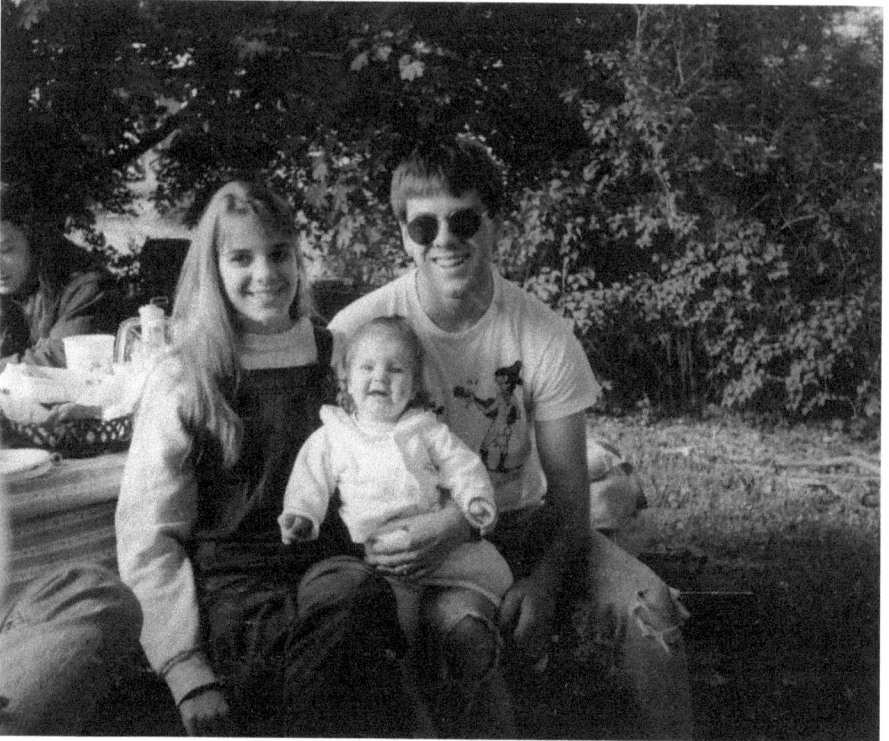

Goldyn age 20, Michael, age 22 & Sweet Baby Jade age 8 months. We found out we were pregnant again when Jade was 7 months old. We rose to the challenge but not without great struggle. Our commitment to never give up on one another kept us going through our hardest times.

Jade age 2 & Kaylee age 6 months. We were babies raising babies.
Building the foundation of our Duffy tribe with love and fortitude.

Michael age 26, Goldyn age 24, Jade age 4, Kaylee age 3. Raising our Duffy girls in style. Creating the foundation of love and strong family bonds.

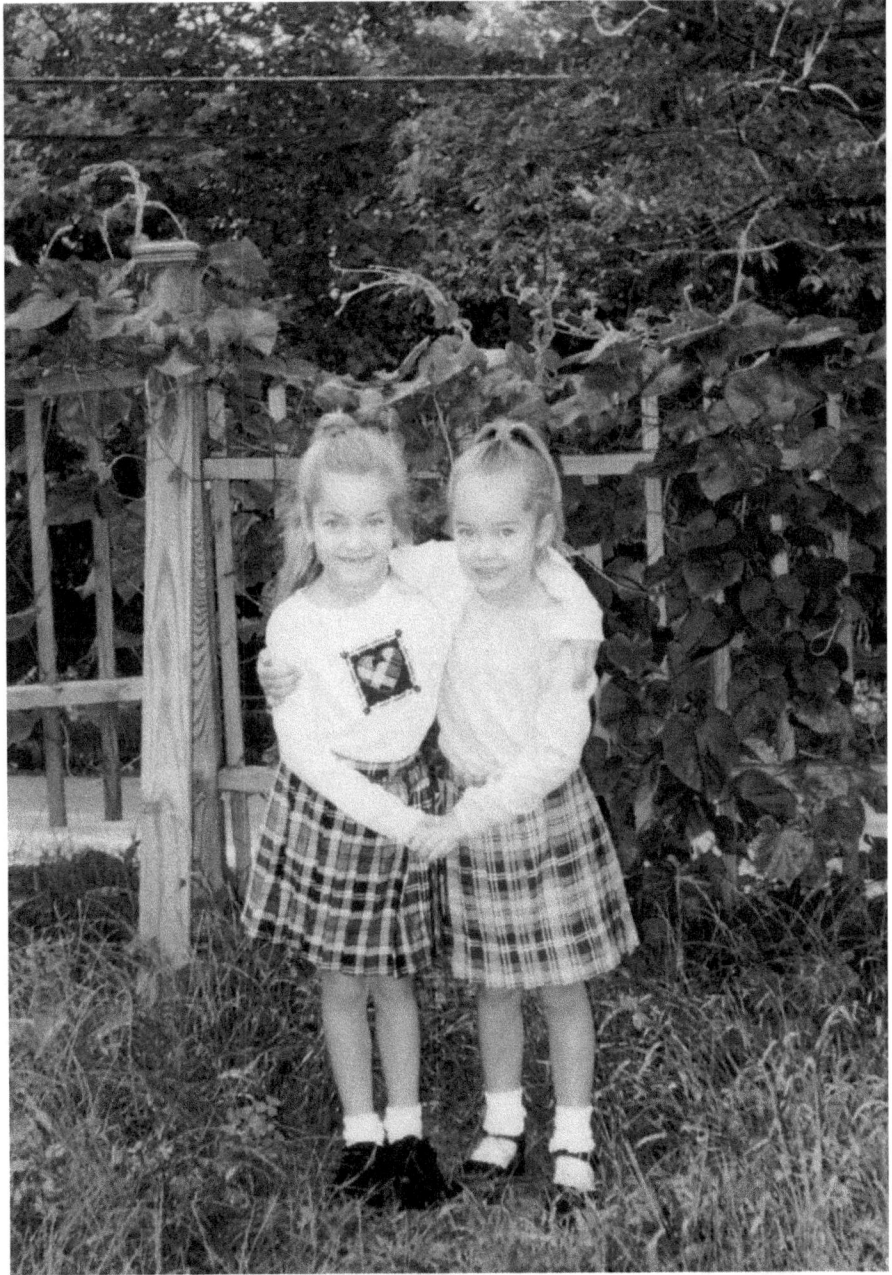

Jade age 5 & Kaylee age 4. They never really knew life without each other and as a result their bond was strong from day one.

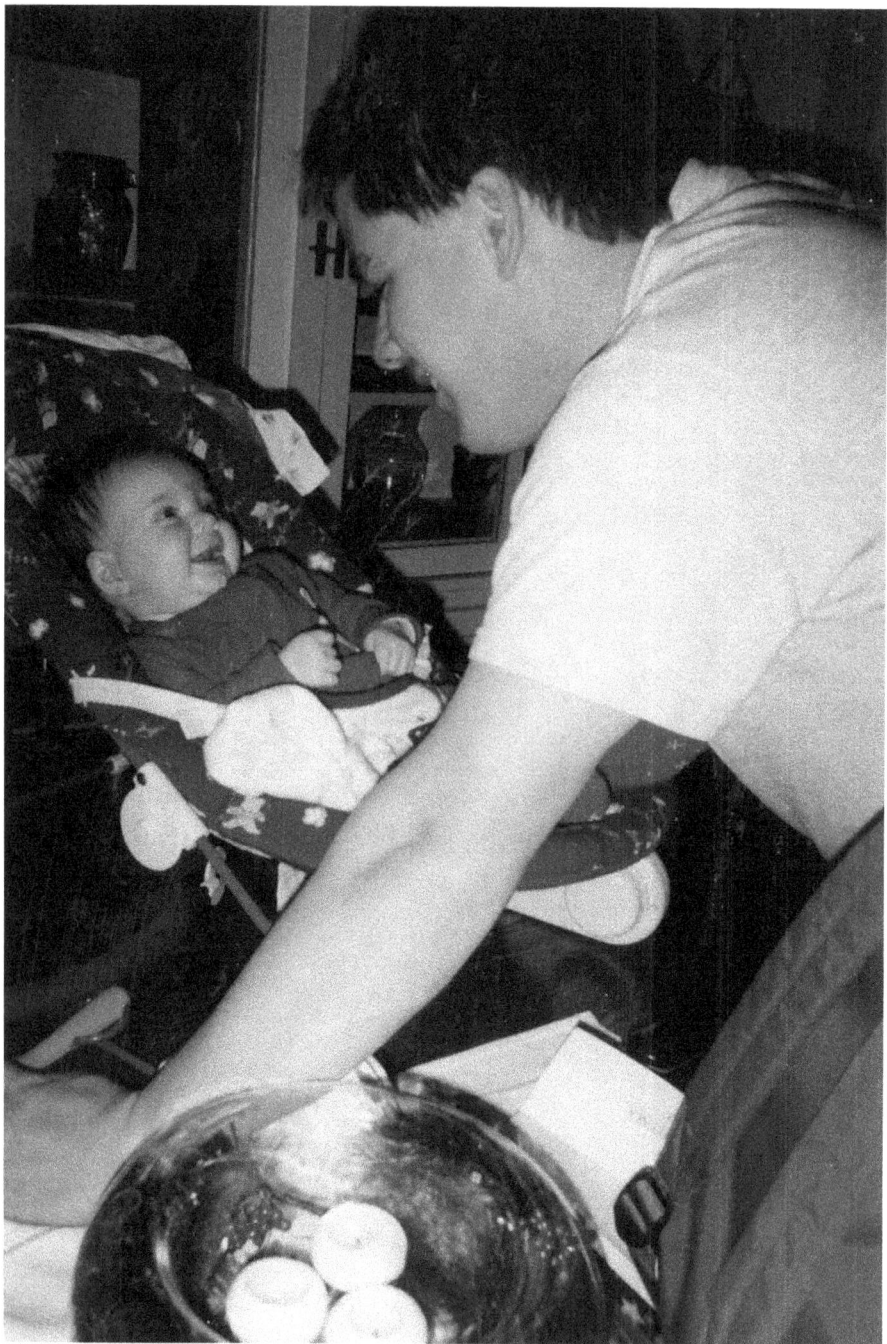

Daddy age 33 & Emma age 4 months. The father daughter relationship when nurtured creates a strong foundation of love and communication. He has always been and still is an amazing father.

Jade age 10, Kaylee age 9, Shaelinn 6 months and Emma 2 years. We never factored that our love would multiply with each child we brought into the world.

Shaelinn, 6 months old. The sweetest baby that completed our Duffy tribe.

Jade age 15, Kaylee age 14, Shaelinn age 3, Emma age 5. Raising teenagers and toddlers created a very strong desire in us to create a peaceful and loving home.

Shaelinn age 7, Emma age 9, Goldyn age 40, Michael age 42, Jade age 20, Kaylee age 18. Capturing a family picture every year is a tradition we hold dear.

Kaylee age 18, Jade age 20, Emma age 11, Shaelinn age 8. Duffy girls, always there for each other, in silliness and joy.

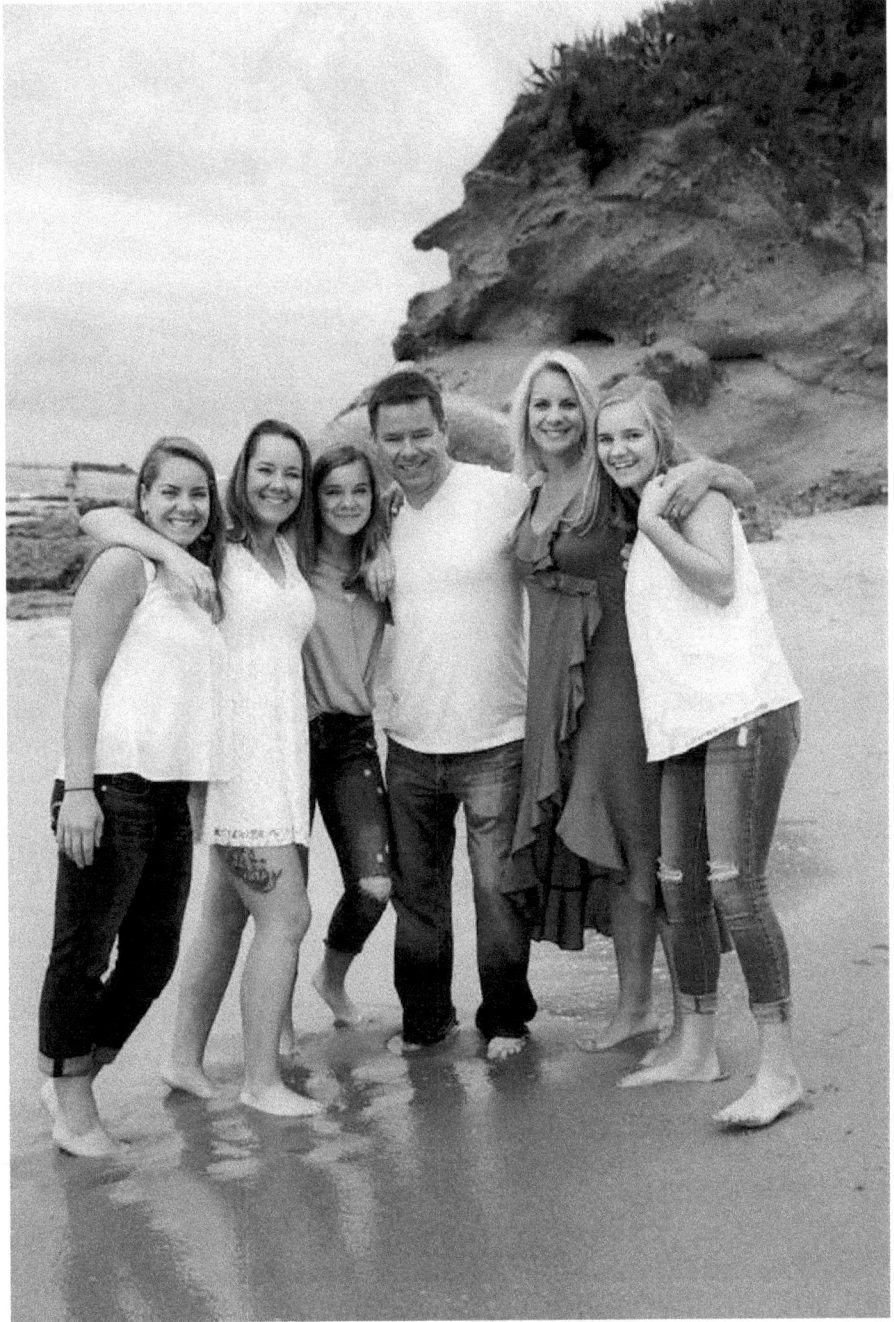

Jade age 25, Kaylee age 23, Shaelinn age 13, Michael age 46, Goldyn age 44. West Coast is the best coast.

Kaylee age 26, Kinsley age 2, Mavis age 2. Creating joy and love in their family.

Shaelinn, Goldyn, Casey, Jade, Michael, Emma, Kaylee, and Kinsley. Our family in 2019 at Jade & Casey's wedding. Our tribe continues to grow in love and joy.

23

FEEDING TIME

So I like to cook and I like when people eat my food. What do you think happens when a parent puts a whole bunch of effort into cooking a nice, healthy meal and a child refuses it, or says it tastes awful and puts a scowl on their face?? It makes you wanna knock their block off. Well, it could be a full out battle or it could be nothing at all. Listen, power struggles with food are incredibly common. It may be the biggest power struggle parents face on the daily. Especially if you have what some would like to label a "picky eater." My third daughter was incredibly picky. She went from eating everything as a baby to eating next to nothing as a toddler. I remember feeling helpless, frustrated, and yes worried that she wasn't eating enough. I would try to get super creative and give her cut up watermelon, cheese and carrots. She lived on peanut butter & jelly dipped in ranch for years. Ewww right? She's eighteen now, still a picky eater and still claims that peanut butter &

jelly dipped in ranch is delicious. The bottom line is your child will not starve and yes they will eat when they're hungry. This same child only needs to eat twice a day so I never force her to eat dinner because she simply isn't hungry. You must trust your child's inner guidance on this one and do not set yourself up for failure by making them eat things they hate or sit at the dinner table after everyone's left. You do not have to let them eat cereal if they don't eat their dinner either. Again, give them choices. Ask that they at least try a bite of what you make and if they hate it, make sure there are always sides they like. A kid who lives on noodles will not die, and eventually he/she will eat a variety of foods later on in life. I mean seriously, think about the crap we grew up on and we survived. In fact, I'm downright healthy despite all the Spaghettio's and TV dinners I ingested.

The truth is your child will go through different growth spurts and at times won't be very hungry and other times will seem like they won't stop eating. It's so important to get them to listen to their own guidance and know when their bodies are full or hungry. If you have a child that seems to be an emotional eater and has taken on extra weight, it's time for some communication about that. Communication, not judgment or insults, or worry. Just a simple conversation around heavy foods and health. If you have a bunch of junk in your house, well then, you may set them up for some bad habits. I eat super healthy and as a result, so do my kids.

I have encountered a child who began disordered eating when she went through her teen years coupled with depression that led to cutting. What I can say about this time is that communication saved the day. We kept the lines open, stayed in solution energy and continued to find things to help her. I found my fear and anxiety the total enemy in this situation and that I had a tendency to make this "all about me". Meaning, my fear that I was a bad mom or did something to cause this in my daughter was the biggest issue. I spent months detaching from the worry and from feeling I had to save her. The bottom line is anything our kids face: they must want to get better and any sort of forcing or resistance makes things worse. We tried energy

77

healers, therapists, shamans, holistic doctors and nutritionists. The truth is I just felt like I needed to do something. I researched eating disorders and realized that I did not want this to be a life sentence for my daughter. I think part of the problem within our society is that we label people and then that label becomes their identity. After meeting with a holistic nutritionist who found lots of heavy metals and toxins in her system, we found a solution. She will now say she HAD anorexia and that gives me great ease. If you research the subject people will say you have it forever and on that note I would say, "you achieve what you believe". This is why I am so careful about labels. I work on not making decisions about who my children are based on circumstances and instead focus on who they are becoming. When you factor in the knowledge that our cells regenerate every seven days, any chronic illness or disease is one that keeps manifesting because of the belief systems we have given it. We give our ailments power when we decide we have no power over them.

24

DETACHMENT

When faced with your own child's struggles it is very easy to take those things personally. To feel as though you have failed them as their parent and guardian to their well being. As you walk this uncertain walk of guiding these young beings through an ever changing world, it is easy at times to lose your footing. To feel fears and anxieties that you didn't even know were possible because now it is up to them to find their way. You can feed them and clothe them and keep them safe, but then they get to decide if they will continue the path of health or not. You can show them the way, give them healthy choices and lead by example but it doesn't mean that they will always choose that path for themselves. Sometimes they will take detours, detours that will make you feel like your heart is being ripped out of your body and you want to scream so loud you hurt your vocal cords. There are feelings, feelings of powerlessness and despair you didn't think were possible for you because you were sure about life, you were sure about deliberate creation and energy and visualizing the best possible life for everyone. As a mother how do you detach? How do you take this little being who you held in your very own body, sacrificing your own well being through years of sleep training, breastfeeding and colds and flus and allow them to experience their own journey? I ask myself this now on a daily basis and I sometimes can grasp it and feel better for a few days and then the fears come back and the anxiety is almost more than I can bare. I talk to a life coach who asks me why I keep making this about me. I don't have an answer for her. The only thing I can say is, "She's my baby, I would die for her." I think it can be very easy for some parents to close down their hearts, refuse to look inside at what they need to heal, but for me it has been my life mission. To heal, to grow and to raise my daughters in the brightest light possible. To show them that life is meant to be lived in joy and no matter what, that joy can be found within. But I'm starting to realize that maybe it's just not that easy. That there are things we are called to that perhaps create a space where joy cannot be found. A place where the darkness is so dark that no light can stream in. Places within our own motherhood that feel completely beyond anything we could have prepared for. When we feel we can't reach them and we don't know where to turn. When we research and the research makes us feel even worse and more scared for their well being. I feel like I'm coming up short. I feel confused and often days out of control. I watch my little girl as she struggles and I just want so badly to take the pain away, and I can't. There is an elephant sitting on my chest throughout the day and 2 a.m. is my time of extreme panic. She asks me why I keep making this about me and the truth is I don't know. I only know that I have always felt my children's pain at a very deep level. I have always struggled when they have struggled and I have always done my very best to be there for them in any way they need me to be. But this is different. This is my baby. It's easier to get lost in her pain because she is my focus. Life is not as busy as it once was and I believe there are even ways in which I feel I have failed her and caused much of the suffering that she is going through. My dream to move across the country brought so many challenges for her as an adolescent that it's easy for me to feel that I made a mistake. That I failed her and took her away from a life that would have meant more happiness and health. I know this is my irrational mind giving me reasons to feel bad and yet it's easy right now to listen. To hear all the awful things I am usually so good at tuning out. In some ways I feel I am sharing her burden but I know deep down that is not true, my pain only makes things harder for her and I know it's not helping to shift her out of this. When we focus so much on the problem and the fear of worse case scenarios we have no chance of finding the solutions. There is a path we must go through. There is pain and healing that must be done because we are *human. The reason why I think this now is because it has felt very much beyond my control to find my footing in all of this. I have moments of real strength and feeling like we are going to get through this to have something then show me that I'm not as strong as I like to think I am. And then I'm back. Back to fear and anxiety like it's my job. In the past I have felt very weary, maybe to the point of surrender, oh if I could just surrender, I've done that a few times too. Why can't I just let go and let God? Where is my faith and why isn't it driving this crazy bus? The things that I know sometimes come into play, I remind myself, I visualize. I see things as working out and everyone as healthy and happy again and then somehow it evaporates without a trace. I find myself then thrown back into the fire of anxiety and terror. A place where I can't get a handle on my thoughts and I feel like they are eating me alive. I reach for help, I look for support and miracles and I always find them. It's enough to keep me going. But the darkness hangs there in my heart, the darkness I imagine she is immersed in, I keep reaching for her. I do my best to only show her love and not my fear, but I often fail. I am sure I am suffering more than is necessary here and yet right now I don't know how to stop it. I'm reaching, reaching within and I can't find the peace that is normally so prevalent for me. I reach for my knowing from all the miracles I have seen and the faith that I have worked on growing through my entire life, I keep coming up short. I am conscious, I am aware, I am a mindfulness teacher for crying out loud and I can't find my center. I feel lost and alone and so, so scared. It's changing me, I can feel my personality changing. I can see the selfishness in this writing, how I have made this all about me and how horrible this is for me. I know that I am taking on more than is necessary and it's not healthy and right now I am not sure what to do about it. I'm so in the problem that the solution cannot come.*

This excerpt is from a time of extreme contrast of walking through depression and disordered eating with one of my daughters. It lasted about seven months and turned all of my philosophies and modalities upside down for a bit. I am happy that I didn't finish this book before we found solutions because the journey was such an important part of our growth and healing as a family.

Things got bad for a time and began to look like we may have to put her in a program to save her life. She lost 45 pounds and was weighing in at 93lbs. She looked drawn and unhealthy. She was beginning to look like a skeleton and like all the scary pictures you see of girls in the hospital starving themselves to death. She was cutting herself and withdrawing socially from all of her friends. She told me daily how much she hated life and didn't want to be here. The struggle was tremendous.

As a parent it is so easy to allow our children's struggles to become our own, to take on so much worry and fear that we can't possibly have any access to the solutions. Many miracles happened at this time and people and books were strategically placed in my life through Divine Intervention. I once again have no doubt and my faith has grown exponentially.

We were looking into many different healing techniques to help her and I was attempting every possible way of getting myself through this without causing further damage or slowing down the energy that could promote her healing faster. It didn't feel right to go the normal route and put her into treatment, my concern with that was what was being taught, that this was a lifelong issue. That once you had an eating disorder it was who you are and you would always struggle with it. Because of what I know about our beliefs create our reality, I did not want to believe that and I did not want her to believe that either. So I decided to consult a psychic. I wanted to know how long this would last and if there was something I could be doing that could help her heal faster. Now it's important to note that up to this point in my life I had never gone to a psychic and being the deliberate creator I am, didn't really put any value on someone telling me the way the future would work out because I believed in creating it. So it was somewhat out of the box for me to do this. The psychic said many things but one thing in particular that confused me was that she asked me if I had ever read anything about the Rowandan Genocide? I said no and she said it was coming up and I may possibly have some work to do with it. She mentioned Immaculee Ilibagiza and suggested that I look her up. I discounted it pretty quickly thinking, "I have no interest in that" and didn't give it another thought. The things the psychic told me made me feel somewhat better but it didn't get the elephant off my chest or give me the cure for my daughter I was so desperately looking for.

One afternoon I was feeling particularly anxious after trying to bring my daughter to a restaurant and her asking to leave immediately. We got in the car and I said "Honey, you have to eat, you don't want to die, do you?" To which she replied, "I really do."

This sent me into a rabbit hole of fear and panic. I went back home and decided that I needed to get out of the house so I went to get my nails done. After I got my nails done, I felt like I couldn't go back home and be alone with my thoughts once again. Sitting in my car I got this very strong intuition to drive over to the bookstore. My guidance said you need to stop being afraid and go read about solutions. So I listened. I walked into the bookstore and felt like my body was being led somewhere. I suddenly found myself standing in front of the book "Live to Tell" by Immaculee Ilibagiza about her experience with the Rowandan Genocide. My jaw dropped. Now this was not a new book and it just happened to be on a shelf facing out where I was standing. I opened the book and the forward was by Wayne Dyer, who I have always felt a very special connection with. I have never met him but always felt very close to him and then he died on my birthday. In his forward, he explains that this is the best book he has ever read on faith and hope. I began to cry right then and there knowing that this book was sent to me to teach me something I needed at this point of my journey.

I immediately bought the book and left the bookstore. Feeling like I still needed to be alone, I went to a spot under a tree at a park that my daughter and I discovered that is incredibly peaceful. I felt gratitude for my guidance but still had no idea why I needed to read this book about a subject I would never have wanted to open my awareness to.

A little time went by and I dedicated my night time reading to this book. It was frightening and horrible what happened to these people and the onslaught of violence that occured to this woman. She was locked inside of an extremely small bathroom with eight other women for three months with only a small plate of food to share every few days. Suddenly it hit me!! This woman lost 65 pounds over this course of time and came out and recovered. I swear this book was showing me that the human body is miraculous and my daughter would heal from all of the damage that was being done. Immaculee also showed me faith at a different level. Literally putting your life into God's hands and then seeing how miracles would take place so that she would survive this tragic time in history and live to tell about it one day, in fact that is the name of her book, "Live to Tell".

The miracle of being led to this book helped me to begin to release so much worry and concern and to surrender into the process of the journey we were going through. It allowed me to give my daughter some space and let her come to her own desire to heal, when she was ready. I was still bringing her to a Nutrition doctor and getting her blood tested and blood pressure checked. We signed her up for therapy and ended up realizing that that was a huge mistake and was only making matters worse. So we stopped the nutritionist and therapy and just gave the whole thing space for a bit. I shifted my energy and asked the Universal Energies to provide us with the assistance we needed to heal what she was going through. I trusted and started to feel my faith strengthen.

At the time, I had met this woman at an event I attended and she became a huge support to me. She would talk to me on the phone and worked on helping me to detach from the experience so I could stop creating more drama. She advised me to look at my daughter's heavy metals in her system and I said yes, and then, just like the book, forgot about it. I had heard celery juice was a good idea but then was warned against it because she didn't need to be detoxing when she was starving herself.

So I let go, I stopped obsessing and I asked for help from the non-physical. I stood in the place of knowing that the right people and information would come and she would fully heal from this. I worked on backing away from the fears and thoughts that had become such a habit that I often felt I had no control over them. I took my power back. I had full faith that a solution was coming and I began to notice a change within my daughter that helped me to see the energy shifting, so I knew I was on the right path.

I decided to go the route of looking for a nutritionist. My daughter began eating but was still restricting and her stomach was a disaster. She suffered from major stomach aches and she was still losing weight because she wasn't eating enough. She said she was open to talking to someone about the right way to feed her body to help it heal. Finally, I found two women on facebook and messaged them both. One of them got back to me right away and we had a discussion. I thought I might give her a try but I waited because I wasn't quite sure about it yet. Essentially it wasn't a hell yes and I usually only go with things that I intuitively feel strongly about. So on the day I was going to message the first woman and let her know we were going to try her out, the second one messaged me and we set up a call. I instantly clicked with her, she said everything I needed to hear. "Hell yes."

We made an appointment right away and started to do muscle testing to see what she needed. At the time, she weighed 93 pounds. Turns out her body was full of heavy metals!! We began a program for her and she started to get better. She was still struggling around the food area and had some depression, so her nutritionist suggested she try a session with a hypnotherapist. Between these two women my daughter was completely cured in two months time. She went back to a healthy weight and no longer struggles with food. She told me that the terrible voice in her head that was telling her not to eat was gone and I truly feel she is free from this.

Research will tell you that eating disorders are incurable. We refused to believe that. The fact of the matter is, whatever you or your child may be diagnosed with is completely curable when you know how to work with Universal Law. I think many girls struggle with eating disorders for so long because we are not addressing the root causes. The idea that they need to feel like they have some control over their lives, I believe, is only partly the cause. My belief now is that heavy metals play a huge factor in mental challenges and when you clean up the internal piece along with helping the subconscious to clear the belief systems attached to it, you have a powerful combination for healing to take place. This worked for us and by working with the energy that we were conducting, helped us to shift the energy that activated solutions and promoted her healing.

I also think it's really important to mention here that any time your child is struggling with something to first understand that it's temporary, and next to understand that it is an important part of their journey. The reason I know this is because of my Higher Perspective awareness that we are here for growth and expansion and we can have faith that all things are working out for us when we believe. By holding on too tightly and desperately trying to find a solution from fear, I could not find it. The problem and the solution have different vibrational energy so when you are too focused on the problem and doing things out of fear, you cannot align with real solutions. It wasn't until I worked through my fears, let go of needing to change things and accepted that this was an important part of our journey, that the solution came. My daughter also needed to be in a state of readiness and that came in her own timing, not according to mine. The journey of parenting is not always easy and there will be times that we will do the wrong things and spend way too much time worrying and fretting about what we do not want. If you have lost your footing in your parenting journey, have faith that it is an important part of your growth and learning to detach from needing your child's life to always go the way you planned.

Understand that they have their own journey here and by being too worried or sad for them, you only disempower and disrespect the growth that they came here to do. Trust in the perfection of their lives to unfold exactly the way it needs to unfold for them to expand and grow into the beings they came here to be.

So whatever it is that you may be facing with your child, take heart in knowing that it will pass if you give it the right sort of attention and put yourself in solution mode. My faith was a huge part of what grew in this situation and the belief and trust that my daughter has her own guidance. As long as I can get her to communicate with me I know we can overcome any challenge whether it be physical or emotional.

25

SIBLING RIVALRY

Nothing could quite turn me into a raging maniac quite like some good old constant sibling squabble. For those of you facing this daily struggle, my heart goes out to you. There were days when I would literally want to pull my hair out and I would sob out of frustration. I would yell at them and separate them and punish them. I could not understand why these little girls hated each other so much. I couldn't understand why everything had to turn into a battle of the wills, including mine. I asked my grandmother what she did and she told me she used to lock her girls in separate closets! I told her you could get arrested for that now. What I realized after much research and experimentation is that most sibling rivalry is rooted in powerlessness. Yes, yours and theirs. Because they feel powerless, they will try to get you on their side and create the most annoying scenarios to get your attention. If you have older ones who are constantly terrorizing your younger ones, you can be sure that they are dealing in powerlessness and maybe a little jealousy. If your kids are close in age and they are fighting, please note that they are learning a ton about social development and navigating relationships. Your best bet against this type of energy in your home is communication. Communicating with each child and making sure that they know you understand. Especially the older ones. We can often set up an unrealistic expectation of our older children and expect them to behave and tolerate certain things way above their maturity level. When we take them aside and let them know that we know their little sis or bro can be super annoying and that we feel for them, they will realize that this is no longer an attack on who they are. They will feel connected to you and like they have some sort of reprieve in just knowing that they are not alone. Helping them to figure out their boundaries and excusing themselves when things get too intense will arm them with a great strategy in life. It's not about avoiding sibling rivalry but instead showing them that they have a choice not to take part in it. I also like to help instill compassion in them to see if they can find anything positive about their sibling to focus on. I explain frequency to them and that big radio station. I let them know that as long as they are focusing on what is annoying them, that more annoying things will come. I think it's super important to teach our kids about their own conduction of energy and how that plays out in their experience. I love putting my kids up to experiments to see what will work for them.

26

YOUNGER KIDS

When it comes to your younger children fighting, the most important thing to work on here is keeping your cool. Keeping yourself out of these situations will ensure that you are not activating more of the drama. I know, it's hard. The fact of the matter is most of the time our children are fighting to get our attention. Most of what they are fighting about has to do with feeling powerless and wanting to matter. Think about it, someone says something you don't like or takes something that belongs to you, how do you respond? As parents we have been taught that sharing is an important part of our child's development and an important part of them navigating the world to play nice. But seriously, sharing kinda sucks, doesn't it? Here you are happy as a clam playing with your doll and you have to share it with your sibling who is younger and careless.

27

SHARING SUCKS

When I was about ten years old, my cousin gave me a gymnastics Barbie. Oh my goodness. I was so in love with this doll, she was more flexible than the average Barbie and she had cool equipment where I could show off her skills. The day I got her, it was insisted upon by my parents that I let my sister, who was a few years younger than me, take a turn with her. I was less than happy about it, but being ten years old, I accepted because I simply had no choice. Well not five minutes into it, my sister broke my new barbie beyond repair. I was absolutely crushed. I couldn't believe that I was forced to do something that ended up in me losing what I had just been so excited about. Maybe this is why I think sharing sucks. But you know what, I still insisted my girls did it and didn't even question the social programming around that until I started to wake up to the trouble with it.

So why do we have to share? I know the belief is we are teaching our children kindness and maybe even a certain level of non attachment for things. There has always been a belief that if we teach our children to share that they will have a greater sense of caring for others, but does that count when we force them to do it and they don't want to? Or does that kind of thinking create resentments in them towards their siblings and others? I can honestly say after my traumatic Barbie experience, I was not a fan of having to share anything and I did not trust my sister to take care of my belongings and never felt inspired to share with her again. I think it's ok to allow our kids to have things that are important to them that they don't need to share. I mean really, as adults how often do we share things that we love or are super important to us? Such a weird concept we have been teaching our children is important. I think it's better to give them a choice. You can help them pick the toys that don't feel so special to them and have those things be the things that they can share. This way they get a sense for sharing and don't create powerlessness or resentments around it.

So what to do when your children are fighting all the time? First of all, communicate. With every one of them separately. Let each child know that you feel for them and help them come up with ways that they can create more peace. Help them to see that you understand their frustration and bolster them up by letting them know that you are on their side. Be sure to spend one on one time with each child so they know they matter to you and that your relationship is important. Back away from getting in the middle of these situations and if your kids are physical then absolutely insist that they separate. I grew up in a house where things were very physical and there was no hard line set against this. My brother knew that physically hurting us was wrong but he had no way of controlling his emotions because he was never taught. He was also hit by my parents quite a bit which further solidified his belief that this was how you dealt with conflict. If you have been hitting your child, I will strongly advise that you stop. My belief that this type of parenting does not work and only further creates a belief in your child that they are powerless. I know that there are parenting books out there that condone it and I did try it when my older girls were little and it did not work. It just showed them that hitting was ok. It showed them that when someone was angry and if they didn't obey, they would be physically punished. Again, this is a dictatorship-type of parenting that will never yield a healthy relationship. Also, I think nowadays it's super easy to get your kids taken away from you for this type of behavior. Kids are no longer quiet about what happens to them at home and social media makes our lives an open book.

Sibling rivalry can be super frustrating, but it doesn't have to be what rules your house. If your kids are being destructive to the energy field of your home, you need to help them manage the emotions and frustration they are feeling. Help them by giving them the tools to navigate the relationship and help each child to create compassion toward the other by opening the communication. I love to have my kids write out lists of things about one another that they like. This helps tune their frequency into the station that is more peaceful. They may not always agree to do this but if you present it as an experiment and maybe even a contest that they can get really good at, you will provide them with a tool they can use their entire lives to improve relationships and the life they live.

Understanding your vibrational set point is very important when we begin to look into what the strongest energy conduction is when you are spending time with your children. So your vibrational set point is your mood. It's how you are feeling and can be based largely on how you are thinking and what you are believing. Do you feel frustrated and annoyed when you are with your children? Do you feel impatient most of the time? Do you live in an expectation that spending time with them is stressful and hard? How you feel about being around your children is the number one reason why it may not be peaceful. You expect it not to be and in that, you tune your frequency into the most annoying radio station on the planet.

28

ADOLESCENTS AND TEENAGERS

Parenting in this age range is where we take on warrior status. You may feel that your home has become a battleground and that you are limping around wounded and explosive. Your child has turned into an unrecognizable monster that you no longer can say anything to that doesn't make their eyes roll back in their heads. Ok so first of all, understand that the brain function of these creatures is similar to what was going on in their heads when they were toddlers. The frontal cortex of their brain, which is where they manage and process emotions, is not quite developed yet. The hormones that they have raging through their bodies is equivalent to a fast, raging river after a huge rainstorm. Meaning, not anything they have control over. They have tons of pressure from peers who now have access to them twenty four seven and the academic pressure alone could turn anyone into a hot mess. **I recognized within my own girls that when**

they were at their absolute worst was when they needed to be loved the most. That the reason they were acting so terribly is because they felt awful inside. Any insistence to tell them they are awful or bitchy is a direct attack that will only make them feel worse. Ladies, has your husband ever told you at that time of the month that you were being a bitch? Did it ever help? What did you really need at that moment? Perhaps a hug would have made you feel better. Think about when you are at your grumpiest, people telling you that you are grumpy never does anything but make you grumpier.

I used to lay in my daughter's bed and think about her life. I would try to put myself in her shoes and imagine what it was like to be her. I would allow myself to feel the pressure she felt and I gained quite a bit of compassion from doing that. I think it's easy to forget that these taller bodied beings are still children. Their brains and hormones are still in a major growth phase and they need to be cut some slack. They need to be shown that when they are at their most unlovable, you will still offer them the love and goodness that they truly are down deep inside. This doesn't mean we become a doormat, it just simply means that we don't judge them and criticize them for behaviors that they have no idea how to manage. If you can get them to talk about their feelings, great. I know some kids may resist this, so in that case, just tell them that you are there for them if they want to talk and that you understand that they are going through stuff. Let them know that you love them no matter what and if they want help managing things you can help them find ways to feel better.

Did you know that it's actually a normal process for our kids to start distancing themselves from us? They have to do this to make the whole leaving the nest thing easier on themselves and us. It's a natural progression for them to create angst in your relationship so they won't be completely heartbroken when they have to leave you. Knowing this may make you wince and feel like there's no hope. But there is, I promise. If you follow my advice and don't take your teens behavior personally, you will navigate this part of your family's life much smoother. Remind yourself daily that they will come back. Keeping in mind that one day your relationship will be better and they will like you again and you will like them again. Look for glimpses into who they really are as much as you can and train your focus as much as possible.

29

TRAIN YOUR FOCUS

In order to change the way you feel about your children, you must learn how to train your focus. This means bypassing your mind and the 60,000 thoughts you have had day in and day out for decades. It means having a practice that helps you disengage from the mind's antics. It also means becoming aware of what your thoughts are before they have the chance to physically manifest. So what's your mood around your kids?? Are you snappy and demanding like a drill sergeant getting marines out of bed? Are you tense and frustrated the second they give you any lip? Can you back away from the habits you have formed within your mind and now manifest on the daily? These are all really important questions because knowing the problem and becoming aware of it doesn't change it. It takes focus and a willingness to change. It takes a commitment to taking care of yourself so that you can show up whole and in a higher vibration to your family.

Ok, so how do you do it? The first step is to notice what your behavior has been around your kids. Write it down. Then write down what you would have to believe to act this way. Notice how your beliefs have been manifesting in your family. Now I know this is hard. I know it can be challenging, even downright upsetting, to step out of victimhood and take full responsibility for the way you have been feeling. The truth is you should be congratulating yourself for even picking up this book and for being this far into it! Ok, now write down each one of your child's names, (you can do this with your spouse too, any relationship really, that you would like to make improvements) and then next to their name write down your absolute most honest feelings about them. Don't worry about being too negative here because we have to be honest in order to release it and create something new. So once you have all those nasty things written down, go to the other side of the paper and write down what you want to feel about your family and then what you would have to believe to feel that way. Write down everything you can think of that you love about your children and your spouse. Reach if you have to. Now the next step is super important. You have to DECIDE that you will focus more on the new beliefs and aspects than what you have been. If you find this challenging then make a list of positive aspects every morning and every night. What this does is tune you into what is good about them. It trains your focus to what you love and therefore you will see more of it.

Here's a great example:

When my youngest was around eight, she had boundless amounts of energy. She had a hard time sitting still and would need to move her body even when we were watching tv. I used to find it super annoying that she would cart wheel around the living room when I was trying to relax and watch tv. Now that she is 15, I would be delighted to see and feel that energy from her. So I decided to write a positive aspects sheet on her to tune my vibration into gratitude and all of the wonderful things that my child was.

Positive Aspects of Shaelinn

I love how beautiful she is and how her face lights up a room

I love how she has amazing energy to cart wheel all over the house and flip over all of the furniture

I love how flexible she is and how gifted she is as a gymnast

I love her energy and her zest for life

I love how much she loves me

I love that she wants me to help her get dressed in the morning and that she still wants to be my little girl (it's true someday your gonna miss this)

By doing this exercise you enable yourself to turn things around with your children that may have previously been annoying you. I remember feeling so done with helping my daughter pick out her clothes, until I wrote that down. I also remember that shortly after I wrote that, she decided she could do it on her own. I now know that this was a sacred time of our lives together and spending extra time with her was never something to dread or regret.

NO TIME IS WASTED AND YES YOU'RE GONNA MISS THIS SOMEDAY

None of your time with your children is wasted. Even when you may feel that they don't appreciate it and maybe even like you are being taken for granted. Everything you do matters and the more you can feel the ease and grace of spending time doing things with your children, the deeper your connection with them will be. My husband and I chose for me to be a stay at home mom because we saw how important it was when we spent time with them. We saw the value in creating a foundation for our children that there would always be someone there for them. Was it easy? Hell no. Did we have to sacrifice a lot? Hell yes. But it has paid off big time. We figured things out financially and always made it work. I lost myself in raising them and would often times feel that I missed my calling to be something other than a free Uber driver. I used to look at the laundry and think, "I have so much more to offer than this pile of laundry." What I can see now is that it was so worth it. I have been able to build a business from home and continue to write most days until my fingers are numb. I am here for my kids when they need me and for us that really has worked. It's definitely not for everyone. If you do work outside the home, you may find it a little more challenging to give your kids the attention that they need. It's important to understand that even if you are not spending a ton of time with them, the time you do spend needs to really be valued. Taking the time to communicate with your child as the full-time working parent becomes even more important because it's easier to be exhausted and distracted by all of your work responsibilities. It's also much easier for you to be burned out so make sure your self-care is on some kind of schedule or you will have absolutely nothing left to offer your children at the end of the day.

30

OPEN THE LINES OF COMMUNICATION

I think we forget that our kids are people. They are living, breathing people who have their own guidance (it's true they really do), and their own preferences in life. They have made their own judgements and perceptions and have decided certain things about who they are and how they are showing up in the world at an extremely young age. Evidence supports that most of our belief systems are formed by the ripe old age of five. Which means many of us are walking around with limited, fearful, five year old belief systems that we have never questioned. One of the biggest issues I see in parenting is that parents are NOT communicating with their kids. They show up as the disciplinarians and create from a corporal general's status that cuts off all lines of communication and creates a feeling of powerlessness and rebellion within their children. Trust me I know because I used to be that parent. Barking commands and demanding respect with no regard for my children's feelings or respecting them at all never lead anyone to any sort of happiness or peace. How can we expect to be given respect if we are in fact being disrespectful ourselves?? Seems crazy right? Well in our defense, I would say most of us are just on automatic pilot and have been programmed to believe that children should just automatically obey their parents. I really don't think this is the most effective way to parent. It may work for you in getting shit done around the house, but how is your relationship with your child? Do you have one? Do you enjoy each other's company? Do they tell you what's going on in their lives? Do they know what's going on in yours? I don't believe we were put in these positions to become their dictators. I believe we are here to form beautiful, loving, healthy relationships with these people. That's right, I said it, people. Your kids are people. Have you ever had a real heart to heart conversation with your child? Have you ever asked them how they are feeling or explained to them why you need help around the house? Have you ever told them that you trust them to do the things you are asking them to do? Have you ever put the ball back in their court?

I was talking with a dad the other day who told me that every night they expect their sixteen year old to turn her phone off at 10 pm. Every night he has to leave the comfort of his couch, pause his show and tell her to turn it off. He told me about the angst and negative energy this was causing. I asked him why he did this. I mean at first I agreed. I think our kids need help with boundaries around their phones, hell even we do. But I asked him why he doesn't trust that she has her own guidance and will do what is right for her. Could he possibly give her a chance to monitor herself? Could he talk to her and tell her why he thinks it's important for her to unplug and give her brain a rest before she tries to fall asleep? When we talk to our kids and help them to see why things are important to us, we actually activate this type of thinking in their experience. When we are acting like the disciplinarian and barking commands they only feel powerless and unheard. This can inspire sneaking around and dishonest behavior. So a discussion is in order and a chance needs to be given to see if she has the guidance to do the right thing for her health. If she wakes up a few mornings feeling tired and groggy because she stayed on her phone in her new found freedom, she will see first hand the consequences of her actions. If we are constantly monitoring our kids, then when they leave the nest they may do all sorts of crazy things because they have never felt this type of freedom before. It's important to activate their guidance now and give them a sense that you trust their guidance, and sometimes allowing them to make mistakes, will help them to begin figuring out what does and doesn't work for them.

31

SOCIAL MEDIA CHALLENGES

When it comes to electronics and our children, I believe we have to come to a whole new understanding about what we are dealing with. This is a new problem and it requires us to get into solution energy. There is no doubt that this challenge has great potential to lead to an addiction within our kids' lives probably more than anything ever. I mean how many of us are addicted? I find myself having to consciously choose throughout my day NOT to look at my phone and I am not always successful at it. It has caused us to no longer be present and to lose communication with our kids like nothing else ever has. We have been given a device that allows us to be constantly distracted. The social media aspect means kids have 24-7 access to one another and small things can turn into big things very quickly. A child's reputation can now be ruined in one click. We are seeing a rise in suicide rates which I think is directly related to this issue. Kids have no escape and they have no idea how to monitor themselves on a forum that is so new to our society. I believe the secret here again is communication. If you can start when they are young to put boundaries around the electronic devices and communicate with your child why it's important to not be on their phones all the time, that could help. If your children are older, I hate to say it's a lost cause but I do think it's much harder and can become quite the power struggle if you insist on putting rules around it after there hasn't been any. For us, we have helped our daughters become conscious about the addiction and what they are subjecting themselves to. Do they still go on their phones too much? Absolutely. Do we? Absolutely. The key to navigating it all is to help your child see that there is life beyond their phone, which means you have to get out and live yours too. I invite my kids to go hiking often or go to the beach so they can get outside and remember what nature was like. They always benefit from this. I do not drag them, I just share with them how important it is and then lead by example. My middle daughter even took herself off of all social media because she could see how unhealthy it was for her and how it gave kids access to her that was not helpful. This is amazing. Talking to your kids about the pressures and false pretenses that the social media world offers is super important so they can begin their own journey of self-monitoring and doing what's right for their well being.

If we don't talk to them about it and we insist on making it a power struggle, it becomes a forbidden fruit. Because of that, they will sneak around and want to do it more. When you have direct lines of communication and create awareness around things, you will always arm your child with the tools they need to thrive when you are not around. By helping them to see the addictive qualities the phone presents and even your own struggles with it, you can come together as a family and find solutions to navigating this new challenge in our society.

If you have kids who are playing video games all the time, I would highly suggest that you monitor the games they are playing and how often they are playing them. Do this at a young age and you will really help them. I would especially like to make you aware that if you are allowing violent video games into your house, you are inviting that energy into your lives. I believe this is a huge contributor to our school shootings and it boggles my mind that people don't talk about video game influencers and only address gun control. Watch the games they are playing and see what kind of feelings you get from them. If we are allowing our children to be desensitized to violence, we are doing them and our society a huge disservice. I truly believe this was what caused the Sandy Hook shooting. The reports were that this boy sat in his basement all day and played violent video games. If you look at this in terms of frequency, when we allow our kids to tune into the frequency range of guns and violence, assimilating killing people, we will tune them into violence on some level. So if it feels violent, I would get rid of it after some real good communication around what you believe these types of games are creating in our society and the potential that these games have on our own energy fields. I would also openly talk to other parents and make them aware of what you have learned about violent video games and protecting our kids energy by not subjecting them to an assimilation of murder.

32

BULLYING

Bullying has been around forever and seems to be quite the epidemic now. Social media has totally upleveled this issue and it seems to be linked to a higher rate of suicide. A few of my girls have had some pretty terrible times in their life due to bullying and to be honest I have been known to approach a few kids, who were bullying my daughter in elementary school, to let them know it wouldn't be tolerated. This has the potential to cause more problems, if you are not talking to kids who respect adults or their opinion. This is easier to do when they are in elementary school. My second daughter was bullied her freshman year of high school because she told on a girl who was smoking pot in the bathroom on her first day of high school. This girl and her friends tortured my daughter for the entire year. We had meetings with the principal and tried to get her parents involved. Looking back, it's easy to see how we were constantly in the problem and just blaming the other girl. This is what I believe kept it going and did not help the situation whatsoever. I am much better about being in solution mode now and if I could do it over again, I would have gone to the girl and opened the lines of communication. I did this for my third daughter in elementary school and it worked like a charm. I talked to the girls that were bullying her and I let them know that it wouldn't be tolerated. I talked to my daughter about her own self-esteem and confidence. Bullying comes from both sides of the fence. The bullies feel powerless and have low self-esteem so they feel like they need to do something in order to feel powerful. Oftentimes they are bullied by their own parents or another student. I can remember being bullied when I was in middle school and I did the same thing to a girl just a year later. I couldn't even relate to her or feel compassion for her because I was totally unconscious and only wanted to feel my power. Remember, I was bullied by my brother so I had to find a way to feel like I had some control over something or someone. My brother was also bullied by my father, so I am sure he had self-esteem issues as well. Someone who is confident and strong in who they are will never be bullied nor will they ever bully. I don't believe this is an issue where kids need to be punished and told they are wrong. I believe this is about empowering our kids and helping them to create consciousness around their actions and the way they treat people. We cannot reach this thing from the surface, we have to help our kids become aware of how they are feeling and then what their actions are creating. And we have to stop bullying them ourselves. By punishing, demanding, commanding and being a disciplinarian, we sever all ties of communication and render our kids powerless. We essentially become bullies. So here's a question: are you a bully?? Do you bully your own kids? Do you have experiences that are calling you to heal so you no longer feel powerless and need to take things out on your kids? I know it seems crazy but I see it all the time. Parents who are overworked and stressed and have nothing left to give their kids can often come across as bullies who take their kids power away and create situations where they need to take their power back somewhere. I truly believe that the issue with bullying really starts at home and needs to be addressed from an inner space. We must help our kids to feel their feelings, address what makes them feel insecure, and help them to grow into decent human beings who don't need to bully people to feel good about themselves.

This issue is not one-sided and doesn't mean we only deal with the ones who are doing the bullying. We also must deal with the child who is constantly being bullied and help them to clean up their internal stories. If they feel powerless, ashamed, bad about themselves and hateful inside, they will attract others to treat them the same. If we were to look at what others are reflecting to us we must look inside and help our children to step into loving themselves and others. By learning to love ourselves, we create new boundaries, new respects and no one can use us as a doormat any longer. This all has to do with energy. When we are energetically firm and strong, no one will even try to mess with us. This doesn't mean we become like the bully, it just means we come from a place of wholeness and knowing who we are. We help our kids to see that there is nothing wrong with them and that they are strong enough to handle anything that comes their way. It would be wise to help them create a list of positive aspects about themselves and start bolstering them up with encouragement and notice what they are doing right. Help them find what they are truly good at. This one step alone would eradicate bullying because when people are confident they do not get bullied or feel like they need to bully anyone else.

33

TUNING INTO GUIDANCE

I think one of the most important jobs we have as parents is helping our children tune into their own guidance. Helping them to listen to their intuition is an integral part to them living the lives they love. The only way I believe we can successfully do this is if we are doing it for ourselves and we are no longer running on automatic pilot in our own lives. So earlier I mentioned quieting your mind and tuning into your own truth through this process. To give you more of a guide in this type of practice, I would ask that you suspend your judgments and beliefs around whether this is possible for you. This may be a whole new concept for you and one that you never considered to be helpful. As an avid meditator and one who has been at it for the better part of 20 years, I can honestly say it is an absolute game changer. Now, you may not have success in getting your children to do this, (the earlier you start the better) but helping them to take deep breaths and get curious to what is going on inside of them is the first step. Just getting them to ask within about how they feel and what feels right for them should be a must in raising them. How many of us have lived our lives just listening and acting from the opinion of others? I have coached many people who could not make a decision to save their lives, and I believe this is the product of always being told what to do and what to think. Now I know life is busy and you may be stressed. Asking your child takes more time and at times you may not have the patience or interest in conducting your family in this manner. That's why your meditation practice will be key in making this successful. If you have a practice you will be calmer, you will have more space to allow things to unfold, and you will have lots of patience to offer that teenager who needs a little time to figure out what her/his internal guidance is telling her/him.

Ok so here's the commitment: for 15-20 minutes per day (your mind is telling you that you don't have time), you will sit and quiet your mind. Taking deep breaths and eventually just letting the breath be normal and finding that space within that is pure bliss. In the beginning this may feel like a battlefield and you may want to throw in the towel. Don't. I promise if you stick with this, you will get better at it. Just commit to sit. Now things may come up. Things that don't feel great and can make you feel things you haven't allowed yourself to feel in a very long time, or maybe ever. Remember you have a whole bunch of social programming going on that has led you to the belief that crying is wrong and negative emotions are to be punished. So funny that we are taught this growing up. Part of our emotional field is stifled and not allowed to be expressed, so we jam it down and put all sorts of stuff on top of it. Alcohol, food, drugs, retail therapy, these are all ways in which we work on suppressing part of who we are. By doing this, we allow a lot of pent up emotions within us and that is why we may feel reactive and have anxiety attacks and depression. All of those things are symptoms of not allowing the energy we are experiencing to be felt or expressed. When you start to go within for the first time, maybe ever, you may experience some deep seeded stuff and need support. Remember we have this awesome community of support and guidance for you to tap into. The M21 Revolution is a great tool to help you

navigate this part of your journey. Here's the link
https://www.facebook.com/groups/M21Revolution/

As you quiet your mind, stuff may come up so do your best to stay
with it, follow it through and stay seated. Allow yourself to come
back to Zero State Awareness, which is the state where all things are
created from. This practice not only allows us to clear old energies but
activates new, fresh energies that help us to get in the receiving mode
in life. It clears the slate for us to begin anew in every moment and
take each day as if it is the fresh, incredibly beautiful journey that it is.
Quieting your mind tunes you into the internal space of joy so that you
may begin creating that in your outer world. Once you feel the bliss
on the inside, it's only a matter of time before your life begins to reflect
the peace and calm that you are connected to, because of your practice
of going within.

34

CREATING A RELATIONSHIP WITH YOURSELF

I know this is a parenting book and not one you thought would help you to work on yourself. I believe that the gift of parenting is just that, a healing for yourself. As you work through this journey with your family and finally admit that things are not perfect, you put yourself in solution mode big time. Your support and intention to work on yourself and heal is the number one most important thing you can do for your family. We cannot create new experiences when we are running on the same neural pathways that our parents lived on. We have to stop the generational cycles by waking ourselves up to the truth. The truth that lies within. The truth that wants to express through you. The truth that brings you back to the awareness that you do have control over your life and you can significantly improve things by deciding that you will stop at nothing to create from your greatest potential.

So commit. Commit to a practice of quieting your mind and notice how things begin to shift. Notice how certain things no longer bother you and that you are able to decide how things will go and then they go that way. Reawaken to the knowing that all things are always working out for you, and before you know it, that will be the reality you are living.

I know it's hard. I know you believe you don't have time, but I'm asking that you let go of that crap and decide that your life's journey is worth this, that you are worth this. That you matter enough to create a relationship with yourself. This is where you will start to uncover the limitless being that you are. This is when you stop believing the lies that you have bought into that no longer serve you. This is where you will awaken within to someone who feels powerful and whole. You deserve this, your family deserves this and it's the most important thing you can do to fully awaken to the power you have within. There is nothing that will help you heal quite like this type of practice. If you really want to wake up, you must go within. If you really want to create a more peaceful family environment, you have to get real about what is going on inside of you that is conducting in your energy field. The traumas and life experiences you have had up until now are still conducting in your life because you have never acknowledged or allowed yourself to release them. This is why you can be going along feeling just fine and someone will say something that will instantly make you feel anger. This is called a trigger and they are always your gateway to healing. If you want to wake up to and release that type of control over your emotional environment you will gain the ability through quieting your mind. If you don't, you will continue the cycles of being a creator by default and life will most likely have it's way with you and not in the most favorable way. If you need assistance, subscribe to www.therealonez.com and you will receive a free training on trauma release to guide you on your journey.

35

ADULT CHILDREN

There are no guarantees in life and there are no guarantees that you will raise your children into healthy, thriving adults or that you will have a great relationship with them. I mean, we hope, right? The fact of the matter is, we are learning and growing along with our children and we will inevitably make mistakes. Sometimes those mistakes will cost us and may negatively affect our relationship with our children. I see many families working to navigate from past wounds and mistakes. I talk to lots of moms who feel guilty and therefore continue the cycle of an unhealthy relationship with their child. Please let go of guilt. It doesn't serve you and it's kind of absurd that you would beat yourself up continually for something you did when you were not even capable of accessing the awareness that you were causing damage. Our children's lives will play out and sometimes they may choose to not have us be apart of them. I know, it sucks and it's hard. It's important to realize that this is an integral part of their own expansion and independence to separate themselves from us. They must do certain things to make that transition easier. The best we can do in these situations is to love our adult children unconditionally and clean up our own stuff. As we clean up our own stuff, we will tune ourselves into a different frequency with them and the ultimate plan is to have a healed, loving and whole relationship. If you have an adult child that reeks havoc and creates a ton of toxic energy in your life, you may have to decide what boundaries will be put in place to navigate that relationship. No one should have that much power over our lives and if your child does, it's time to make a change. Unless you are happy with it. Some people like the drama and truly get something from it, so no judgment here if that works for you. But if you are someone who has recently raised your vibe and now you are finding it tough to tolerate an adult child that just likes to activate drama, I would like to give you a pass to free yourself from a lifetime of struggle by limiting the access they have inside of your head and your life.

It is totally possible to stay in a relationship with them as long as your boundaries are in place and you can do quite a bit of accepting about who they are and the way they create in their lives. If you cannot accept them, then the urge to change them will shadow the whole relationship and cause lots of lack that will not help change the situation. If you can back away from it and look at it from a Higher Perspective, you will be able to see that your adult child's journey is their own to create.

There are so many things that we face as parents that we may feel powerless about. One that comes to mind is drug use. If your child is an addict and has promised over and over again that they will quit, and has made a mess of your life and theirs, it's time to accept that you may need to create boundaries so that they can hit rock bottom and get help. Their drug use is not your fault and is not something that you need to feel responsible for or guilty about. If they have chosen this life path, it's time to set yourself free. Acceptance is the first step and then setting up the boundaries you need to not allow this toxic habit to bleed over into your life is next. If they have stolen from you, broken promises, and made a complete mess of what could have been a great life for them, it's time to back away. To let them know that you will never give up on them and that you will love them unconditionally but you will not sacrifice your life for the poor choices they are making. This is absolutely heart wrenching as a parent. There comes a time that you need to save yourself in order to live a life that feels good to you. Just because you brought this child into the world does not mean you have signed up for a life of deception, addiction and lies. So you must ask yourself if you are receiving anymore joy from this adult child or not. Unconditional love does not mean we allow our lives to be sucked dry by our children. It means we love them no matter what. It means we let them know that we will always be there for them but that we love ourselves enough to not allow someone else's choice to be destructive or destroy us. I know this isn't a cut and dry case and it gives you an even more important reason to quiet your mind and get clear inside your heart. When you are fully healed and whole inside, you will feel the unconditional love that will either help transform the relationship or allow you to let it go until your child wakes up and stops choosing the chaos.

I am incredibly thankful that none of my children ever got involved in serious drugs. I can only speak to this from an experience I had for a brief time with a boy I love as much as one of my children.

Here's the story:

So one night back when we lived in Connecticut, we were having a going away party for our second daughter who was moving out to Arizona. Before the party she had shared with me that a friend from school was really struggling with drugs and depression. When he showed up at the party, I knew I needed to talk with him and see if there was anything I could do to help him get his power back. We left the craziness of the party to sit on the front porch and talk. We talked for two hours. He shared with me that he was still living home, going to college and absolutely hating his life. The only relief he got was from drinking alcohol and doing drugs. At this time, he told me he was no longer doing drugs because he had almost overdosed and learned his lesson. He was 20 years old and did not have his driver's license or a job. He told me his parents refused to help him and he felt depressed and stuck. We came up with a plan that he would start working for my husband and because he lived right down the street he could ride with him to the job site everyday. After a month or so of this working out he decided to leave his parents home because it was a negative place and he felt unsupported. He started living in an environment with friends who were doing drugs and he told me he didn't feel it was the best place for him and asked if he could move in with me. We had an extra bedroom and agreed that he could stay with us and pay us rent. He moved in and it was like he belonged with us. We had family dinners and created memories together. He got along really well with our two younger daughters to the point that they started calling him their brother. He was a really hard worker and I could tell my husband loved having him around. It was easy and it felt like he belonged in our family. I helped him get his license and create a feeling of independence. This was in the beginning phase of us planning our move to California, and one morning I asked him if he would join us in our move. He told me he already had plans to move to California, so we all got very excited. Over the course of the next few months we visited California while he stayed home with the girls. We worked on our plans but nothing looked like it was happening and he got super impatient. He then told us he was going to California before winter started and he would hook up with us if and whenever we got there.

Once he moved, we lost touch. I heard through the grapevine that he was doing drugs again and it made me sad. My hope was that once we were all back together, he would straighten out again. We lost touch for a few years and every once in awhile he would message me. I could tell he was on stuff and I even figured out that he was homeless. It made my heart sad but he's not my child and I wasn't about to invite that into our situation when we were navigating our move to California and working hard to create success there.

One day he showed up on my daughter's doorstep in Arizona when she was two weeks from having her first child. He created a bunch of problems there with her boyfriend and she was so distraught with him being there that we offered to send him a bus ticket so he could come and stay with us. When I went to go pick him up, I didn't even recognize him. He had lost about 75 pounds, had long hair down the middle of his back and he was definitely homeless. I brought him home and the reunion was strained and awkward. He started working for my husband and we worked on getting to know him again. He was definitely not the same person. He listened to super dark music and oftentimes would disappear for the night. I had to go to Arizona for a few weeks to help my daughter with my new grandbaby and left my husband to deal with this boy who was totally off. His stay with us was stressful. We communicated with him and hoped and prayed that he was no longer doing drugs. He swore to us that he wasn't. I did not know that just three weeks prior to him coming to stay with us, he was doing heroin. He and I talked a lot and we started exercising. I could see the light coming back in his eyes. He would have episodes though. He would be good for a week or two and then disappear. He would tell us stories and say someone roofied him and he didn't know where he ended up and didn't want to talk about it. After that particular night, he was so distraught that he cut off all of his hair and swore he wasn't EVER going to drink or do drugs again. He started to seem like his old self again. He worked and read, and started to laugh again. I was so hopeful. And then another episode. I woke up one morning and he wasn't in his bed. I think one of the worst parts was waking up in the morning and having no idea what I would find. We were very stressed and I'm not sure why we did it for as long as we did. So that morning, I came downstairs and he was outside. He was acting so weird. He was standing up against the table resting his head on the umbrella and just swaying back and forth, almost falling over. I called to him and he came to me and I said, "What did you do?" He was crying and hugging me and saying he was sorry. He claimed that his ex-girlfriend (the one he used to do heroin with) had died from an overdose and he was just really upset. Well, I'm no dummy and could tell as he was nodding out on the couch, that he was absolutely out of his mind on drugs. I told him he could no longer stay here like this and he chose to leave. The crazy thing is, my husband did not want to give up on him and still allowed him to show up and go to work. He was homeless and sleeping in the woods. We gave him a pillow and a blanket and felt nauseated about the whole situation. He chose to stay outside because he couldn't commit to staying off drugs. That wasn't my choice but it still felt awful that I had a home and I couldn't let him sleep in it. After about two weeks of this, he came back around and showed up at a high school football game that we were attending. I realized at the game that he was having trouble seeing. After inviting him back to the house for dinner, I asked him if he would stay again under the stipulation that he would not do any drugs. He agreed and the next day we took him to get some new glasses. He borrowed the money from us and paid us back by working. This seemed to create a change in him. He could see again and he seemed so much happier and his vibe was higher. He started talking about his future and how he wanted to get a place. He had misplaced his license and told me he wanted to go to DMV to get a new one. He seemed like a changed man. He was no longer drinking and he was exercising and eating super healthy. He put on some weight and felt like the boy I remembered being willing to help. I was so hopeful. Once again we felt like a family, started creating memories and even had a trip planned to the Grand Canyon and invited him to join us. One morning he asked me if I could take him to the DMV to get his license again. He had borrowed money from my husband and bought a motorcycle and was anxious to become independent again and get on the road. This whole situation kind of terrified me. I really was not in the space of trusting him or thinking his independence was a good idea. Everytime we would attempt to go out and leave him alone he would have an episode. But it had been a few weeks and he seemed like he was doing so well that I offered him my car so I could get things done and not have to sit at DMV with him. He called me throughout the day and kept telling me the line was so long and he was just waiting. It looked like he wouldn't make it back in time for me to get the girls from school so I Ubered to DMV to get my car and even brought him a sandwich because he said he was starving. When I brought him the sandwich he seemed a little off but I thought it was the excitement of getting his license and I brushed it off. When I came back to pick him up a few hours later there was definitely something very wrong. Again, he was out of his mind. I felt crushed. I totally lost hope. I made the decision that I was done. Now, I know he is not my child so I don't know what it would be like if he was, but I can tell you I had an uncommon love for this boy and it made it very hard to give up on him. He had turned our lives upside down and made us feel like we were trapped into taking care of him. But on this day, I had had enough. I told my husband that I couldn't do it anymore and he agreed. After watching this boy completely out of his mind again, my husband lost his cool. He yelled at him and told him he was disappointed and that he couldn't believe he was throwing this opportunity away. We let him stay the night and then told him he would need to leave in the morning. He chose to leave that night. No apology, no thanks, no nothing. I was completely heart broken. A few days after he left, he sent me a text asking me to leave his belongings out and then he kept checking to see if his license had arrived. It was taking forever and I was feeling super bothered that he was homeless in my town and I might see him. My heart was broken and he didn't seem to care. I listened to Russell Brandt's book, *Recovery*, to try to understand the addicts mind and how they work. Turns out addicts don't have the capacity to think of others when they are in the midst of their addiction. That was evident. His license never came and I got a message from someone that he had left California and was back in Connecticut. I was absolutely furious that he didn't let me know he was leaving and I sent him a long text letting him know what he had done to our relationship. I also let him know that I would never stop loving him and that I hoped that he would get the help he needed to heal. He never responded. I'm pretty sure he blocked me after that and blocked me on Facebook. That really hurt. It's not that I needed thanks or even an apology, it just felt like we turned our family's life upside down for no reason.

I've heard through the grapevine that he joined the Air Force. I have seen pictures of him and he looks really good. It makes my heart hurt when I look into his eyes and imagine how he must feel for hurting the two people who loved him so much. I hope he does well, and I hope he never returns to the life that was clearly so destructive.

So even though these few months pale in comparison to a parent who is facing this type of destruction with their own child, I believe that it gave me a little window into that world. I have so much compassion for any parent facing this and I will use my intuition and guidance to share what I have found in this brief moment navigating this with someone. I know that the person who has turned their life over to these highly addictive drugs is not the same person they were before they started. I know that they think differently and it causes them to act in ways that they have no regard for anyone else. I know that these drugs have the potential to steal someone's soul and to have them live an existence that is a far cry from who they really are. I'm not ecstatic over time spent with an addict but I am glad that I know first hand what it's like in case I can offer any insight to someone who is struggling. I also think it may have been a good message to my teenagers who felt like they lost their brother to something they would never entertain getting involved with.

The truth is we cannot sacrifice our life for anyone else. If we do, we all lose. In order to survive this type of experience, I believe you need strong boundaries and self-love. The healed parent who deals with the child addict will be so much more equipped to navigate this without feeling like your whole life has been taken away.

36

LETTING GO

I think the hardest thing I have encountered as a parent is letting go. Realizing that our children have their own journeys and must encounter and walk through their own struggles is not an easy task. Again, it is not taught so how are we supposed to know how to deal with it. I have worked really hard on detachment, but not until after creating a lot of heartbreak for myself and contributing to the struggles with my children.

The truth is we spend so many years being completely responsible for these little beings, giving them everything they need and hopefully helping them create a wonderful life, to one day just having to let them go. I mean countless hours are spent ensuring their wellbeing with no guarantee that what we are doing is appreciated or even correct. As they grow into teenagers and then into young adults we are expected to just be ok with their decisions to navigate life in the way they are being called to. There is rarely any regard for what we think or how we feel. This is where detachment becomes super important. We must release from the role of being their savior and now just be the loving, unconditional support we apparently signed up for. This is not easy but I promise it is doable. The more we fight and resist it the harder this transition is for everyone.

My third daughter is currently getting ready to go into the Marine's. I can't tell you how many people have told me I am crazy for letting her do that. Let her? Excuse me? She has a calling that I cannot deny. We have talked to her at length about this and for the last year of her life she has completely had her mind made up. It would be incredibly wrong of us to insist on her denying the guidance she has within. The bottom line is, we are not always going to be thrilled by what our children choose and if we want to maintain a healthy relationship with them we must just continue to give them loving support. I take myself to the end of her marine journey to help soothe my anxiety about it. I picture myself at her graduation and see the pride and strength in her eyes. I'm not always good at it and I'm sure I will have more work to do once she leaves, but I'm not causing any unnecessary drama in the meantime.

Whatever your child chooses, your best bet in maintaining a healthy relationship is to listen to them and create an understanding about who they are and who they are becoming. Giving them the space they need to grow and learn is an integral part of raising strong, independent people. By showing them that you believe in them and their dreams, you will be giving them a strong springboard to launch from.

When they fail and make mistakes, maybe about things we have even warned them about, it is very easy to feel anger and disappointment. The heaviness of these two emotions will never lead us down the path of compassion or love. It is our job to process through our emotions before we become reactive to things they may have chosen. Often times our children may choose and fail at dreams that felt so important to us. We may become vested in their plans and feel like there is no other way for them to be successful unless they complete the plan. This type of thinking will set you up for a very rough road. It's so crazy to think that we must support them in everything they decide and then if they decide it's not working for them to support them further. There are, of course, boundaries that need to be put in place and consequences for all actions because if we are always trying to save them from the pain of their mistakes, they will never learn. Everything they are experiencing is an important part of their path and what they are being called to do in the moment. If they get down the road and find out they made a horribly wrong decision, it's no longer up to us to make them feel like a loser or point out their bad decision making process. This can be hard, but it doesn't have to be impossible. The trick is to pull back from your experiences with your child and remind yourself that no matter what you are facing it's ok. There is always a way to find the Higher Perspective when we take a step back from our fears and disappointment and allow our wisdom to come through. Here is a text message between my husband and myself after our daughter's journey with the Marines abruptly ended.

Me: The disappointment within my heart is so heavy and when I ask why it's because of the unreasonable expectations I have for our child to be something that she is not. It's standing in all of her faults and the ways I feel I have failed her to get her through an adversity which I know nothing about. It's my deepest fears of my children doing things that I feel I have no power in. Living their own lives, listening to the call of what is good for their heart and soul. From Higher Perspective we are doing a good job and to look at this experience as she is less than her potential is a very far cry from the amazing being that she is. To not create further damage we have to heal this part of ourselves and realize that the journey is exactly as it was designed to be.

Michael: I agree with all of it. I want to heal my disappointment in her before I see or talk to her so I don't cause further damage. She is an amazing being and I see so much more potential in her than I think she sees in herself. That is why it hurts so much. So many thoughts…. Just trying to let them flow for now and not grabbing ahold of any of them for too long. I will see where it lands. I have decided not to work tomorrow and to spend the day in nature, in the quiet.

This was an integral part of our process after one of our child's plans ended in failure. But was it a failure?? Maybe by the world's standards but if we look at life through the lens of living a life we love and one that brings us joy, then haven't we taught her to listen to that call no matter what the cost? How many people do we know that have given up what they truly wanted to do to please their parents or some society programming?? Then they get to 40-50 years old and find out everything they have worked so hard for is making them completely miserable. Mid-life crisis anyone?

We have to loosen the reins on what we think is best for our children and start listening to what they feel is best for them. And let's face it sometimes their plans suck. Sometimes their plans break our hearts and cause them to move 1000's of miles away from us, causing the ultimate feeling of detachment and yes, maybe even a bucket load full of disappointment. Our pain is our invitation to heal and to detach ourselves from telling someone what to do once they get to the age of making decisions for themselves. Our trigger of pain affords us the ability to go within and see where we have given away too much of our power and set ourselves up for expectations that things need to work out in a certain way for us to be happy. Let's stop leaving our happiness up to other people and take back what is rightfully ours by trusting their journey to unfold as it should.

37

WHEN THEY LEAVE THE NEST

I truly believe the hardest thing about parenting is learning how to let go. To allow these beings who you have raised, fed, kept safe, and spent their entire life making sure their needs are met, to become who they are meant to become. To not hold them back and instead to let go in a way that lets them know you are there for them, and that you support their journey whether you agree with it or not. Even if it's not part of what you thought would be best for them. I have news for you, you are not them and you do not know what's truly best for them. They have their own guidance, their own passions and their own understanding about what brings them joy. They did not grow up with your fears, your perspectives or your point of view. They have their own agendas, own callings and their own desires. I think that one of the hardest parts of this parenting game is this "letting go when it's time." I don't think anyone told us how hard that would be, in fact no one really says much about how incredibly hard parenting is. Our society just insists that we should all do it as the natural progression of our lives. I wonder how many of us would have gone through with it if we really knew how hard it would be! Probably why that's a big, fat secret. I would do it again because I know that no matter how hard it is, there is nothing like seeing your child grow into an amazing adult. Watching them grow and expand into amazing people is super rewarding. There is no feeling quite like loving your child and seeing what incredible people they become. Truly, it makes it all worth it. My adult girls have always been the light at the end of the teenage/adolescent tunnel for me and when they were teenagers it was my little ones that would help soften the blow of knowing my teens were pulling away and becoming independent.

Right now I am facing my last two children leaving the nest. My third daughter is in her Senior Year of High School and has decided to join the Marines as soon as she graduates. This came as quite a surprise to me and a major blow to my heart. For weeks I have been in denial, not really believing that she was serious, and today I am beginning to feel the full capacity of her really going. My husband always says, "The trouble with raising strong, independent women, is raising strong independent women." So right now I am working within my emotional field on accepting and letting go. This is not easy by any means and no one tells you about how much this will hurt. I often reflect back on my own journey and when I started to pull away from my parents. I think about the way I used to feel and how my mom and I bickered for the last few years before I left home. I moved out as soon as I finished high school and I never went back. That is actually considered success in the parenting game and one that can make you feel, as a parent, that your heart has been ripped out. I remember with my oldest daughter, who I have always gotten along quite well with, not being able to stand her the last year she lived at home. Everything she did got on my nerves and I wasn't quiet about it. Knowing that this is a natural progression in their development and an important part of them being able to leave us has definitely helped me. Now with my third daughter, I am starting to see how I am constantly pecking at her and how she is being super reactive to everything I say.

I am watching in a very highly aware state and I can see how this is part of the natural progression of letting her go. If she is getting on my nerves all the time, then it's much easier to let her go follow her passions and move away from home. Such an interesting concept. I believe the snarky teens' purpose is to help us to let go and not be totally traumatized when they leave us. I am actively participating in moving away from those thoughts and words that cause angst in our relationship. It is not easy and it takes work. I am watching what I am allowing myself to get annoyed about and I am consciously choosing to stay away from my old beliefs around the behaviors I find less than enjoyable. I totally know deep in my heart that the moody teenage attitude is not truly who my baby girl is and sometimes I catch glimpses of that sweet little girl who used to think I was the greatest thing next to sliced bread.

My husband continually reminds me of how we have empowered our daughters and that has made them strong women with strong desires. We have fueled them to live life to the fullest and to pursue what they are feeling called to go after. It's such a good thing but it doesn't make it hurt any less.

The truth is some days no matter how awake or how aware we are, this shit is gonna hurt. If we allow ourselves to lean into the hurt and not take it out on our almost adult child, we will create a stronger bond in our relationship with them and help ourselves in the process. I remember when my older two were young adults and deciding that I would no longer nag them. I thought about the fact that this was not what I wanted them to remember about me and I made the very healthy decision to stop worrying about stuff that didn't matter. I realized that picking up dishes from their rooms or helping to contain their stuff to their rooms, only took a few minutes of my time and was not worth the battle. I know, I know, we want our kids to be responsible and to manage their own belongings, but the truth is they are watching us and will most likely model our behavior (hopefully this is a good thing) once they leave the nest. Being neat and organized has always been a thing of mine. It is very easy to see how much smoother our houses run when things are in their place and we are not going crazy looking for things. I do believe that in the past I have caused way too much negative energy in being worried about the cleanliness of the house for my family. I realize that if I want the house to be clean, it's pretty much up to me to keep things organized. I can ask for help, but the minute I become intolerant or demanding is the minute the house becomes filled with an energy that I am not interested in creating.

38

GRANDPARENTING

I refer to this as THE BEST THING EVER. I absolutely love being a grandparent. I believe it is the cleanest love on the planet. Grandbaby love is close to the love you feel for your own child, yet you do not have the expectations and pressure of actually being the parent. My energy is so different towards my grandbaby that I am able to pay attention to it and allow it to be one of absolute unconditional and high vibrational love. I do believe we need boundaries with our adult children as parents as much as any other time. If you have given up your life to care for your grandchildren, then I am not one to say that is wrong. However, I have decided that that is not the role that I want to play and one that does not serve my life of joy. I love having her when she visits and knowing that I do not see her every day helps me to stay in full appreciation of her and our relationship. When we are together, it is pure bliss and she knows the boundaries of what she can and cannot do by my energy. The bottom line in grandparenting and in all things in life, is making sure you are feeling joy. The minute something feels like a burden or you don't have a choice, you have taken a powerless position that will only create more reasons to feel powerless. I personally do not want anything clouding my relationship with my grandbaby and that is why I am super aware and conscious when things become too heavy. Pay attention to the way you feel and if you are not feeling good, go within and address it. Decide what you want to happen next and with compassion and love explain to your adult children what you need to ensure that this grandparenting thing is the most possible fun it can be.

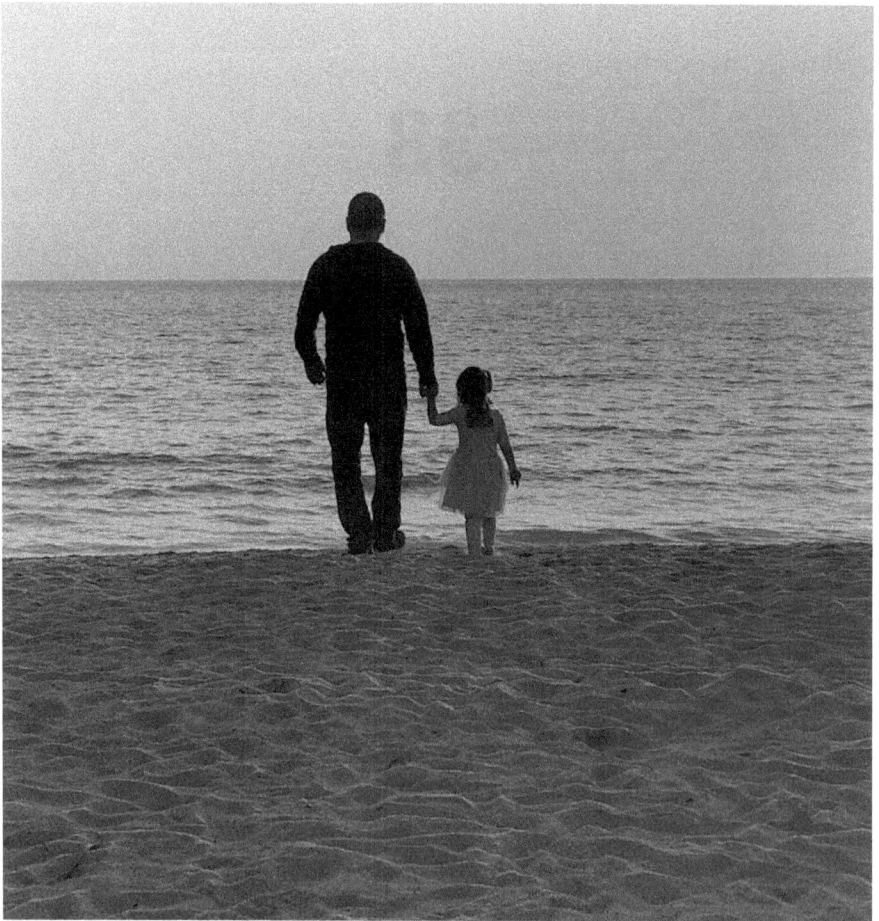

Michael and our grandbaby Kinsley. The best thing ever.

39

ELDERLY PARENTS

I had to include this part in this book because I believe it's an important part of what some of us may be facing. Right now we are looking at having my father-in-law stay with us who is having health issues that is affecting his ability to live on his own. I offered for him to stay with us because it was in my heart to do so. I do not claim responsibility for him. I only know that I love this person and I am willing to walk this part of his life with him. I think it's really important to understand that if you are going to agree to care for an elderly parent, that you do it with really clean energy and all the compassion your heart can muster. If not and you offer this out of resentment, obligation and burdensome energy, you will set yourself up for a very painful journey. A journey that will feel heavy and daunting.

Realize that our elderly relatives are now looking from the outside in.

In the past they had busy, exciting lives, now they are in a position to just watch us from the sidelines and allow us to love and support them from an attitude of grace and appreciation. When you look at it as an honor to provide space from a loving place, you keep your energy focused on the highest state available.

When it comes to walking with someone through the end of their life, we have the unique opportunity of loving and supporting someone who needs us. When we love and trust that our journey is unfolding with information and gifts to help us grow and expand, we can take each thing that we go through and see its fullest potential. When we allow our faith to show us the way and answer the call of our hearts, each experience becomes richer than the last.

40

BE EASY ON YOURSELF

So the parenting game is a challenge and it may just be the biggest challenge of your life. Navigating relationships and our own triggers within them is all just a calling to heal. If we can get ourselves out of victimhood and start taking responsibility for the frequency we are emitting, we will become much better at creating our own realities. Make a commitment to yourself and your family that you will stop at nothing to tune into the frequency of peace and joy in your home and your entire life. As you focus on this journey and the healing you are being called to do, you will see first hand how important and life changing it is. By learning the strategies that I have presented, you have invited back your power. I'm happy to say there's no going back now. Will you be perfect from this day forward? Hell no. But you will be more aware and conscious about the energetic world in which you live. Once you commit to a "quieting your mind" practice, you will gain control over the mind and have more say over what happens in your life. The most important thing to remember is that you are on a journey, one that will help you gather information and grow exponentially. It's in those hard times when you feel you have fallen short that the most progress is made. So let go of guilt, shame and any other self-criticism you have been using to keep yourself from your own healing. Quiet the voice of your inner critic and instead start asking what needs to be healed. Pay attention. Be gentle. And know that this is a process of deep reflection and awareness that will assist you in finding your true strength and wholeness within.

About Goldyn Duffy

Goldyn began her lifelong mission of becoming a mom at the early age of 19. As she and her husband Michael navigated being young parents and creating a wonderful, happy and peaceful life for their family, they had many challenges along the way. Once discovering Universal Law and their own path to inner peace, they realized how incredibly effective this was for their family. Their lives ultimately became so much more peaceful and they could see the joy they were able to create by applying the principles Goldyn shares in this book. Goldyn is the wife of Michael Duffy for the past 27 years, mother to four daughters and Gigi to her grandbaby. She is the author of Quantum Speak, where she teaches readers the science and spirituality of manifesting. She is the co-creator of M21 Revolution, alongside Jess Gumkowski which is a mindfulness community that supports practices to quiet the mind and teaches Universal Law & Yogic philosophies. She is also the co-creator of The Real Onez alongside Lisa Jones, where she teaches real life principles on manifesting and creating your best life. You can find their show on Facebook or Youtube. Goldyn also runs retreats worldwide and helps participants to go within and step into their power to become master manifestors. She lives with her husband, two of her daughters and her two kitties in Southern California.

www.ingramcontent.com/pod-product-compliance
Lightning Source LLC
Chambersburg PA
CBHW072352090426
42741CB00012B/3011